When Bae Is A Demon

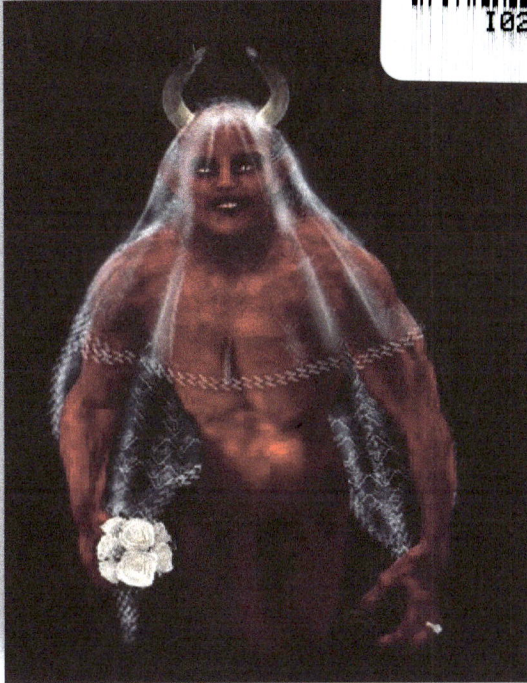

Power Must Change Hands

Markeida Faithe, LICSW

"The Power Pusher"

Copyright © 2022 Markeida Faithe

ISBN:9781736860441

Special Dedication

This book is dedicated to all of the viable men and women of God with spiritual Baes, who are seeking and expecting the fulfillment of one of their heart's desires, a spouse. Accept this book as an offering de-signed to bring your troubled but hopeful hearts hope. Accept this book as an offering designed to equip you with strategy to defeat the nagging spir-itual blockage. May your testimony soon be, in the names of Jesus, "I woke up and broke up with the enemy to my marital destiny." May your vocal decla-ration strengthen as you shout from the mountain top, "Kingdom marriage is my portion." As you walk down the matrimony aisle, may your testimony be, "God did it for me and He'll do it for you too."

Introduction

Just in case you snagged this book thinking that I'm co-signing with you that your past or current Bae is a spawn of Satan, I am not 😊. This book is written to address and educate Christians regarding demonic entities who claim unsuspecting and suspecting hu-mans as their love interests and complicate their path to marital bliss. For the sake of pop culture, I refer to them as, demonic Baes. Most call them incu-bus/succubus or spirit spouses. The majority explor-ing this book are quite aware of what I'm referring to. You're here looking for information that will help secure your spiritual freedom and I'm pleased to an-nounce that you're in the right place. No worries, even if you chose this book with the wrong under-standing, you too are in the right place.

I openly admit that the topic of demonic Baes is not an easy one to discuss within and outside of the four walls of the Christian church. As a result, scores of believers remain ignorant and under un-necessary bondage. So please, do not feel ashamed if you suspect that you are yoked in an evil marriage with a demonic Bae, this is the time to target and end its rulership. Your ability to permanently eradicate his attachment to your life rests solely upon your understanding of what it will cost you in time, focus and your resolve to fight until you've acquired victo-ry on earth as it is in heaven. This book contains eve-rything vital that you need to know to strategically and permanently dismantle and disavow your de-monic Bae's claim to your life. I'm confessing up-front that most will not win this battle but you can! The results rests purely on you and your determina-tion to demand that power changes hands.

Writing this book brought conviction into my life that the fight to destroy a demonic Bae cannot be primarily about attracting an earthly husband but rather, eradicating the works of a devil who's claim-ing you as his Bae and blocking the benefits of your true husbandman, God. Of course, this is not literal as some religious fanatics paint it out to be. You are not literally married to God. Your marriage to God is symbolic. It's a spiritual marriage with spiritual ben-efits that manifest into natural benefits. If you make this fight solely about getting an earthly Bae, you're going to miss the divine point and fall short of spir-itual success. And as a result, power that rightfully belongs to you and God will never change hands.

The demand for power to change hands is about securing and protecting the position and bene-fits given to you by your heavenly-husband. The church is Christ's bride and the church consists of those who have given their lives to God. These are they that Christ will present to his father at the end of time (John 6:39). In 2 Corinthians 11:2, God made his intent quite clear concerning the church. He did not mince words concerning how deep His affection for His bride runs. If you were ever confused about how God feels about your demonic Bae, the follow-ing scripture provides incredible insight:

2 I am jealous for you with a godly jealousy. I prom-ised you to one husband, to Christ, so that I might present you as a pure virgin to him.

Perhaps your main drive for picking up this book is indeed your drive to break into your marital destiny or attain peace in your current marital cove-nant. I've got you and God has you even the more! I would like for you to shift a bit and make God your main drive and His benefits your sub drive. God knows that you desire marriage and one of the beau-tiful gifts of your heavenly husband is the awarding of an earthly husband or wife. Marriage is a fruit-benefit of God's. Readers, focus on and minister to the vine and the fruit will come. Bank on it.

For your Maker is your husband—the LORD Al-mighty is his name—the Holy One of Israel is your Redeemer; he is called the God of all the earth. Isiah 54:5

Satan hates the institution of marriage but go-ing even further, he hates ALL THINGS GOD! Satan aims to contaminate the bride of Christ (church) so that she can become defiled, undesirable and ulti-mately, rejected by God because sin cannot stand in His presence. Satan goes to and fro seeking whom he can devour (1 Peter 5:8), so be alert and of a sober mind because it's not a game. This is the main job of demonic Baes; they spiritually defile their subjects of affection.

The two most powerful covenants that a per-son can enter into involves blood and sex. Satan does nothing without sex, so under his bridal covenant, you are going to get sexually violated in one form or another! It's nothing for him to use someone to mo-lest, rape, coerce you to fornicate or seduce you with one of his resources such as porn. Even if he couldn't physically touch you in childhood, he waits patiently for the willing to choose fornication. And while waiting, for many, he sows his tares while they sleep (Matthew 13:25). This is where most sexual dreams have their root.

The originator of nothing good and original wants so very badly to be like God. He wants a bride (followers) even if she's a pseudo bride so that he can present her to himself; for his glory. He's noth-ing like Christ. He's pure liquid evil. He doesn't cov-er, protect or provide for his bride. He wouldn't dare give his life for her. Instead, he abuses her and drains her of all things God and that's WHY you can't afford to allow him to claim you as his Bae.

Christ came so that you can have life and have it more abundantly but Satan comes only to steal, kill and destroy (John 10:10). Christ gives: love, grace, mercy, laughter, joy, healing, prosperity, fruit of the womb, honor, lessons for growth, acceptance, strate-gy, no limits, success, lofty ideas, inventions, strength, might, intelligence, power to attain wealth, settlement, a future and hope. Satan infects his Bae with degradation such as: delay, setbacks, stagna-tion, limbo, humility, dishonor, shame, rejection, jealousy, envy, strife, sickness and disease, poverty, almost but not enough, barrenness, death, decay and a demonic Bae. He takes from you and gives to his own.

Demonic Baes are no respecter of persons. They do not discriminate. They claim the weakest to the mightiest and the thinnest to the thickest. They rock with all races, nationalities, genders and faiths. They don't care if you are a believer or non-believer. They want the upper hand over a person's life by any means necessary. Yes, it's true, they especially love men and women of the gospel of Jesus Christ because of their hatred for God. What they are de-pending on is your ignorance, compliance and lack of motivation to fight back. The enemy is banking on you being easy.

I have no interest in legalism or trying to scare you. I realize that this is not a topic that you can cas-ually chat about with just any one. I had several de-monic Baes and it was HELL getting rid of them. So I'm not writing as a spectator but as an overcomer. I will give it to you straight. If you intend on living a John 10:10 life, it will never happen while rocking a demonic Bae. You NEED IT GONE. Enough chatting about it. If you're going to chat about it, do some-thing about it! You should not be comfortable with a human or demonic Bae trailing your life and harass-ing your destiny. So STOP crying and running. Turn around and get down with the get down. In other words, FIGHT!

This book will help you face your enemy with confidence. So don't let this be another book that you use just to gather info and dust. Take this book and the information therein seriously. All of the relevant information and answers that you need to demand that power changes hands are here. Stop vainly chas-ing info and THIS DAY, draw a line in the sand through Christ Jesus and declare, *power must change hands.*

Do not be afraid of what you have dominion over. Do not accept what Christ died for you to crush under his authority. Take your power back. Current-ly, your demonic Bae has the upper hand but power MUST change hands. Evil marriages have stopped many. If not dealt with, they will nullify your pray-ers and Finish you. Lift your hands and declare, *"Not My Portion! When Bae is a demon, power must change hands!"*

Table of Contents

Disclaimer

If you have ever been molested, raped, violated, par-ticipated in deviant sexual acts, cover yourself with the blood of Jesus, play some anointed gospel music (preferably a blood song) before delving in. Demons of perversion are strong and they will attempt to manifest in or on your body in a sexual way in order to distract you and further defile you. When you are a host to a demonic Bae, you will fight the urge to become sexual, so be sober and alert. If you feel the urge for sex arise within you, STOP and immediately send the fire of God and blood of Jesus to them. Don't move on until the desire leaves. FIGHTING BACK STARTS NOW.

Two Are Better Than One

While standing sheepishly in the center of an assem-bly of angry women from all walks of life, tears in-terrupted the rhythm and volume of my voice. They surrounded me and walked in a circle like we used to do as children whilst playing Ring Around the Ro-sie. Except, they were shouting one word, and one word only, over and over again, "Idol, idol, idol." My voice trembled as I expressed to the throng of wom-en whose attention I held, how discouraged I was with waiting to be found by a suitable mate. In the dream, my heart throbbed as I spilled from the depths of my soul how I felt forgotten by God. For years, I had been very careful to keep my marital pe-tition before him while ensuring that my desire for marriage did not become my idol. Obviously, the mob of women were accusing me of making my de-sire to get married an idol and I refused to come into agreement with their judgement.

Let me tell y'all, the spirit realm is so exciting and unpredictable. Suddenly, the tone of my voice strengthened and heightened as I addressed the as-sembly of women.

Playing on my love for British and old English culture, I seemingly traveled back in time and addressed the crowd like I was in the mid-century royal courts. If only I could write in a British accent to drive the point home. I cannot but I invite you to let your imagination travel. because in the dream my flow of my words and posture certainly did.

Marriage Isn't My Idol

Noble women, lend me your ears. Do not dare chat-ter that my desire for a husbandman is dishonorable and idolatrous. I assure you, my fair ladies, it is not. I've taken notice to what most of you are afraid to admit and to the ailing belief that has escaped you, TWAIN ARE BETTER THAN ONE. I desire to inter-twine the most intimate aspects of my existence with a husbandman and for that, I shan't ever be ashamed. If marriage is my idol, then what of the Holy word? Was my fair lady with the issue of blood's desperate pursuit for healing, her idol? Doest thou inform me that her turbulent drive for healing was idolatrous? My ladies, look thou not perplexed, the answer is NAY. Healing was her God blessed birthright. Healing was what she saw in the heavens and wrestled to pull down into the reality of time.

She ran to the man whom she perceived could change her life for the greater. Did she not interrupt his flow by touching the hem of his garment and usurping virtue from Him? Why yes, so much so that he paused and inquired, "Who touched me?" Take deep inspection. The Healer did not chastise her.

14

My fair lady didn't stop to ask for permission because she knew the heart of the King and that was all the permission she needed. Exorcism from evil and wholeness became her divine portion. My country-man, that's not idol worship, that's called, TAKING IT BY FORCE! So, I bid you, mock me and judge me if thou mayest but examine, am I not worthy of touch-ing the hem of the King's garment? What should it matter to you what I beseech the king to do for me? I ask nothing of you. I have no business with you. There is no cause to quarrel. This is between He and I. When I examine my marital woes, I see bondage.

Power Must Change Hands

I guess the spirit realm tired of my Caucasian herit-age and decided to pump up the volume by calling forth the African in me. And no, that doesn't include calling on African angels. Ha! The dream shifted and I took on a more militant posture. I started pumping my fist in the air while yelling, "I decree and declare this day that power must and will change hands." And when I made THAT declaration, the royal trumpeters blew with all of their might signaling approval and the mouths of my accusers burst into flames and the flames jumped into my hands, indi-cating, the transference of power from one hand to another.

When I arose from my slumber, I knew that my dream was divine and had been sent to arouse me to keep the faith even in the presence of my naysayers. My dream kicked my faith into a higher gear of supernatural confidence that I've not since released. This chapter is vital because before you delve into eradicating your demonic Bae, your mind-set and posture has to be RIGHT. You must become militant in your belief that power must change hands. You must be determined and sure that mar-riage is your portion. Any doubt that you entertain from yourself, the media, statistics or verbal naysay-ers in the forms of friends, family and even church members will operate like the little foxes that spoil the vineyards (Song of Solomon 2:15) or yeast that works through dough deflating its ability to rise (Ga-latians 5:7-10).

Tunnel Vision

I'm here to confront you. What are your truest thoughts concerning marriage? Stop looking at yes-terday and others who just can't seem to get it right. Give yourself permission to get tunnel vision. I'm here to help you get your mind right and to help re-ignite your faith. Father reminded me to REFUSE agreement with anything that speaks a contrary end-ing to the one that He promised me and I'm passing the advice on to you. And that also includes any in-ternal conflict that causes you to waver under disap-pointment and the wait.

Brothers and sisters, pump up the volume and hear me well, if they aren't speaking the heart of God over your marital destiny, shut them down. I gathered that it's my responsibility to verbally cast down all accusations and misconceptions exalted against the truths of God concerning my life and so it is for you. No one is going to guard nor war for your marital destiny like you will. If you want power to change hands, first, check your mindset. You can't be easily swayed by the wind. Every time that you come into agreement with negativity concerning your mar-ital destiny, you affect your marital destiny clock. Stop adding time, resetting or pausing your clock. As far as people go, if they are bold enough to speak against your convictions, be bold enough to chal-lenge or dismiss them. Yes, it's really that serious.

Speak the Word & Rebel

I also observed in the dream that it's part of the pro-cess that my resilience and faith would be put to the test and that it would take the word of God to shut the mouths of the lions. If you want to shut folk up and power to change hands, speak the word. If you want to shut down demons and demand power to change hands, speak the word. What does the word of God say about your marital destiny? What is God's opinion on the matter? If you don't know, you ain't ready to challenge your demonic Bae to release his power back into the hands of God.

Finally, embedded in the Bible story detailing the life of the woman with the issue of blood was inspi-ration to rebel against what had me bent over. Yaaaas, rebel against anything that has you bent over. So Rise up soldier because power must change hands! Just like the woman with the issue of blood was bent over with her blood problem for twelve years, I too had been bent over for many years con-cerning my marital destiny and the woes of trying to make it happen while fighting a demonic Bae. Chile Boo! You'd best believe that Sis had exhausted every-thing possible to attain a remedy and so had I. Dur-ing those long years, prayers ascended before the throne of God that may have seemed like they were going nowhere. Can you imagine how many sacrific-es the woman with the blood issue presented to God? Personally, I can tell you that I offered many consecration seasons, years of fasting off and on laced with declarations supported by faith and I got nowhere! WHEW! I meant well and I gave up on God a few times along the way. I blamed him for my delay because I didn't understand that I had a de-monic Bae. Like I said, I meant well but my problem had been misdiagnosed. Therefore, my treatment plan was not as effective as I had expected. Come on somebody.

A set time

What's encouraging is that in the realm of the spirit, God heard her, answered her and predestined a set time for her deliverance and wholeness. And yes, it was deliverance because when she touched Jesus, whatever had her bent over had to dry up and flee. She was not only delivered but made whole. Faithe's translation: not only did her demon leave, she also received instant inner healing. Through her prayers, she not only gained heaven's attention but heaven's direct answer that manifested itself at the appointed time. Sister girl refused to give up in spite of her stubborn problem. And so it was for me and so it has to be for you. Could it be that this book is your "set time" answer to breaking the limitations that have been placed around your marital destiny? Even so, don't forget what I wrote in the introduction, "This fight isn't solely about you attracting your earthly Bae. The demand for power to change hands is about securing and protecting the position and benefits given to you by your heavenly husband!"

Your Imagination

A quote from Dr. Cindy Trimm in her book, Com-manding Your Morning, stirred my spirit in a way that pushed me back on track after a slew of ministry related difficulties. "Whatever can be imagined al-ready exists; it simply exists in another dimension, in another form or substance and this is the source of all inspiration." I had read the book several times years ago but twenty-twenty proved within the first quarter to be a force to be reckoned with. So much so that everything about my validity in the earth realm was under scrutiny by myself. And instead of sink-ing into a dark hole, God sent me back to resources that initially helped to birth and mature the Power Pusher's ministry. While reading Dr. Trimm's anointed words, I was able to see clearly how spirit-ually undeveloped I was when first introduced to her ministry and how much I had since matured. So much so that as I read her words once more, I was in a better position to see and receive deeper than what the surface words offered. I got the revelation that everything that I could imagine, was God's YES to me and that includes marriage and the many other things that I have before Him.

I am a dreamer. I have a wild imagination but I never made the connection that my imagination is God's preview of coming attractions as Uncle Steve Harvey so colorfully articulated in one of his motiva-tional videos. Everything that I am believing God for and everything that you are believing God for is rest-ing in another realm and it is up to us to pull it down into the realm of the natural. And that's the im-portance of knowledge and strategy.

What good is it to see it and believe for what you see without the know how to unlock the entry gates that can make it yours? Food for thought, I first saw you reading this book in my imagination. I had to go through the necessary steps to pull it down from the realm of my imagination into the natural. I pray that you are tracking with me! Even as I write, the country is on lock down because of the corona-virus. However, in the realm of the spirit, I see this book floating from hand to hand, home to home, church to church, state to state, country to country. I see myself traveling the globe teaching from this gem and helping countless men and women of God break free. I see it, therefore, it must come to pass.

Over the years, my blood-line strongman has appeared to me and threatened to kill me with his gun. In every single appearance, my posture remained the same as he pointed his gun at me, I ain't dying because my work on earth is un-done. Tell me reader, what is it that you see and know in the realm of the spirit? THAT is what you must reach up and pull down in the name of Jesus!

Locate the Lie

It doesn't make sense for your to read this book if you truly can't see yourself in a relationship with a Bae who is not a demon or being used by one. You will do yourself a great disservice if you rush through this chapter and book because you just want answers. If you rush through this book, you will at-tempt to rush through eliminating your unwanted Bae. I will tell you now that's it's not going to hap-pen easily. It takes discipline and a corrected mind-set to eliminate Bae, the demon. You will never break free from anything without FIRST breaking free in your mind. And in order to break free in your mind, you have to first identify the truth in order to locate the lie. Truth number one: power must change hands. Therefore, the lie resides in the belief that your demonic Bae has power. He doesn't. He hi-jacked God's power that He gave to you in Luke 10:19. Professed Christian, what are you going to do about that?!

When Jesus walked into the garden seeking Adam and Eve after their fall, He called out to them and they said, "We are hiding." He inquired, "Why are you hiding?" And they stated that they were hiding because they were naked. All that they communicat-ed was true but the lie was that they needed to hide from God because of their truth. So amazing because it's not like God didn't already know that they were naked and feeling shame.

And so it is for you. Why are some of you ashamed and hiding from your truth? God knows your heart no matter how hard you try to deny the desire or overcompensate in order to prove that you're content single when you truly aren't. Own your truth that marriage is your desire. And cast down the lies, that it's not your portion and that it's too late for you. Throw away the lie that it will never happen for you. Get delivered from the mindset that you're washed up and have made too many bad rela-tional choices. Challenge the lie that a respectable man or woman will never desire you because you're bent over in some areas. Who isn't? Cast down the biggest lie of them all that God doesn't care about your desire to get married. Those are lies that cripple you from dreaming and imagining a God alternative to all that's troubling you.

Let This Sizzle In Your Spirit

I'm like your mother with magnified hearing and yes, I can hear you complaining about being in pray-er for a long time but nothing seems to be breaking but your heart. Although God already knew what was going on with Adam and Eve, he specializes in asking the right questions in order to get the right answers. He desired them to speak their truth out loud. And when they did, our well prepared God was released to initiate plan B, the plan of redemp-tion. God is your plan of redemption. He admon-ished me to remind you that your desire to get mar-ried originated from His heart. Therefore, it truly honors Him to honor himself by putting a beautiful smile on your face and ring on your finger. As one of my most favorite comedians like to say, "Let that sizzle in your spirit!"

Let it sizzle in your spirit that marriage is your portion. If you can imagine it, then it's time to shift into position to pull it down. Let this sizzle in your spirit, you are not fighting for victory but from a place of victory. You are not trying to attain the vic-tory, you already have the victory. If your Bae is a demon, it only means that Satan is challenging your victory! No worries, I will teach you how to handle him.

The Heart of the Matter

Obviously, you picked up this book because some-thing about the title caught your attention and that's great. As I mentioned earlier, perhaps you chose it because your current Bae or former Bae acted or acts more like a demon than angel so the title peaked your interest. Perhaps you knew right away that I was referring to the spirit spouse. Whatever your reason, it's important that you examine your motive behind ridding yourself of your demonic Bae. Once again, if your number one reason is so that you can get married, you are shopping with the wrong mo-tives. You don't need deliverance from your demonic Bae to get married. However, you do need it if you desire to attract and marry Kingdom.

I'm going to drive this point in the ground be-fore moving on because your motives matter. Your number one reason for getting rid of your demonic Bae should and must be because it does not belong in the life of a blood washed believer. Jesus conquered death, hell and the grave in order to give you the au-thority by virtue of His name to break free from any-thing cynical that attaches itself to you. Regardless of whether you desire marriage or not, as a blood bought believer, nothing cynical, nothing dark, and nothing demonic has a right to call you Bae. Power must change hands.

Journey with me through the remainder of this book. You will be introduced to some very inter-esting and embellished characters and details for the purpose of hiding identities. Nevertheless, the sto-ries are based on true events and are being shared with the sole purpose of helping you understand just how real the spirit realm is and to reassure you that you are not crazy or imagining your fight.

You Already Have a Bae

The clock informed me that I had a measly five minutes to log into my computer and connect with my 3:00 client. I was rushing and I had an attitude. I had just dropped my friend Grier off at the airport and I was not happy. Grier was headed to Nigeria to connect with her fiancé, Guvnah, and to meet her fu-ture-in-laws. Under normal circumstances, I would have been ecstatic. Not in this case, Grier is a babe in Christ and her fiancé is a first-generation Christian breaking with tradition from a long and very power-ful lineage of sangomas. Needless to say, Guvnah's family is not thrilled to meet her. However, my beautiful and cheerful friend insists that her smile and radiant personality can win them over. I argued with her for hours that what she was up against was no miss congeniality competition. She needed to ar-mor up spiritually. She just didn't get it. Guvnah did inform her that she was going to experience another type of evil. He then downplayed it by reassuring her that he would protect her. His confidence irritat-ed me because he can't protect her with his words and well-meaning heart. My advice is that they both need to ensure that they are spiritually ready for the spiritual challenge before them. Although Guvnah left before Grier, he had not been back home since giving his life to Christ and renouncing his family's lineage of witchcraft. As a matter of fact, his family knows nothing of his conversion. All that they know is that Grier is a Jesus lover and her presence dis-turbs their family idol.

I begged Guvnah to introduce Grier at a later time but being the prideful and macho-Nigerian that he is, he told me to butt out and that I did. Well, at least from talking to him about the matter. Yup, I'm that type of friend. I cornered Grier and poured as much spiritual warfare knowledge as I could into her. I took her through Power Pusher boot camp. She was an excellent student but ready, I'm not so sure. God, I'm praying that she isn't walking into a trap. Lord, please keep my mind stable and focused on you because I don't want to think negatively. I discern that Guvnah is a good man and he truly loves Grier. He's confident but so naive. He's going back to the village where his idolatrous family is feared and revered because of their dark power. The village shrine sits on their land. His family and the villagers make sacrifices to their idol religiously. What's going to happen when he stands before the family elders and informs them that he renounces the gods that they worship and fear?

Before Grier left, we made sure that we secured a way for us to connect at any given moment. Not only is she my roommate, she's my friend and I'm loyal to her. I'm concerned that she's so excited to change her last name that she's not concerned enough to weigh the demons that the change will attract. Ever since she met Guvnah, her dreams have been off the chain. They have been filled with dark-ness that I will later elaborate on. For now, I gotta make this call to my client.

The Call

I slammed my laptop down and opened it with haste and made all of the necessary connections. I was not surprised that my client was in place and ready to go. I took a deep breath, pushed my con-cerns regarding Grier to the back burner and intro-duced myself. Hi, I'm minister Faithe, the Power Pusher. How might I assist you today? Before I could utter another word, my client went in! Before ven-turing further, I'm delighted to share that it was my coaching call with her that spun a series of events that propelled me to write this book.

Client: Frustrated! Frustrated and discouraged is what I am and I can no longer hide it. I have been praying and living righteously for some time now and I can't seem to attract a man who will take me seriously. I am attractive by my own admission and the admission of others. I am financially stable, fit and I live life to the fullest. Yes, I am spiritual. I have a beautiful relationship with God. He is my life. I am cognizant of God's place in my life. And that's what adds insult to injury. I am so devoted to Him but He doesn't seem to be as devoted to answering my one petition, to be found by my God-ordained spouse. Don't misunderstand me, I'm not saying that mar-riage is the only petition that I have before God. All of my prayers, and I do mean all of them, get an-swered. And that's how I know for sure that my prayers are ascending to the throne. However, it's that one whopper of a prayer request that seems to go unanswered and I just don't understand why.

Look, I'm not getting any younger and I have that itch downstairs if you catch my drift. I am pretty much the only Believer in my family and let's just say, all of the marriages are jacked up or we don't get married at all. You can only imagine the kinds of ad-vice that I'm getting from my highly sexual family members. Power Pusher, I don't have it in me to spread my legs to random men. I don't have it in me to sleep with married men. Masturbation and por-nography are not gratifying nor desirable. Just like Juanita Bynum mentioned in, No More Sheets, I want biceps and triceps lying next to me at night. I want different from what the ladies in my family are comfortable with. I want and need the consistent and stable comfort and company of someone other than my dog, family and friends. There is a void and longing in my soul that they can't fill. And no, Jesus can't fill it either. That's not His role. And before you go there, I am happy and content with myself and I also understand that there is no perfect man and I am surely not perfect. This is not what this meeting is about.

The Cry of My Spirit

Frankly, I'm tired of the church sisters and mothers down playing my desire for marriage. They keep tell-ing me to just get busy for Jesus and that I will be found. It is my respect and love for God that keeps me from yelling, SHUT UP, ALREADY! In spiritual theory, I understand what they are trying to say but their generic advice does not remedy the cry of my spirit that something is wrong. And instead of get-ting upset with women who in most cases are single, unhappily married or just simply don't know what to say, I withdraw out of frustration and cry.

I promise myself that I will not bring the con-versation of marriage up again but the topic seems to arise at every cell meeting or as the women gather after church chatting and each time, I somehow for-get to lock my guard into place and I get naked in the presence of my sisters in Christ. Maybe I subcon-sciously hope that one of those vulnerable moments will reward my transparency and that God would use one of them to speak into my situation with clar-ity. Instead, by the time that the Saints get through with me, I always walk away feeling ashamed and condemned for desiring the very first institution de-signed and implemented by God, marriage.

I keep saying that I must get to a place of si-lence and quiet confidence but my spirit keeps prompting me that I'm overlooking something. I re-member going to my pastor inquiring why he places so much attention on those who are already married while neglecting the singles and he responded, "Do you want their problems?" Huh? Whatever that meant. So I limped away once again left to ascend to the throne room of God, crawl in his lap, and sob while vowing to never desire marriage again, need-less to say, I always left His presence supernaturally charged with more hope that things would soon change for me.

It recently hit me. Why can believers be af-firmed in believing for a house, car or for more mon-ey without ridicule? Why isn't the person seeking prayer for such things told to get busy for Jesus and it will happen for them? Why aren't those same per-sons told that seeking such things is a lack of self-love? Instead, the Saints gather around and go to bat for them in prayer. Why is it easier to help a person believe for material possessions over a believing spouse that will help build the Kingdom of God, family, society and ultimately, the church?

Two Can Chase Ten Thousand

Power Pusher, I am living my best life but it surely doesn't eradicate my desire for love. Love takes my accomplishments to another plane of enjoyment. It is in splendor that I embrace the scripture, one can chase one thousand but two can chase ten thousand (Deuteronomy 32:30). It is in love that I believe God when he stated that two are better than one, because they have a good return for their labor: if either of them falls down, one can help the other up. But pity anyone who falls and has no one to help them up. Also, if two lie down together, they will keep warm. But how can one keep warm alone? Though one may be overpowered, two can defend themselves. A cord of three strands is not quickly broken (Ecclesiastes 4:9-12). I believe God over the error and ignorance of some of the Saints. I believe God over my fears and current relational reality. I believe that God can and will eliminate the Pharaoh standing between me and my man of God. And yes, I am boldly speaking what I desire and KNOW I can have.

Lonely

I dream of the day of chasing ten thousand with the man who loves God more than me. I'm fighting. My marital destiny is important. I am lonely and I will not allow anyone to react to me as if I've cursed when I use the word, lonely. I love God and I love myself. I am lonely for companionship. I'm lonely for the man who specializes in Antoinette. I need his affirmation, validation and presence in my life. Oth-ers may be just fine resting in chronic singleness but I am not. I have peacefully embraced and enjoyed many seasons of singleness but I am now past that point. I desire to enter into a meaningful and viable relationship with a man who loves God and is look-ing for a wife. It matters to me and it matters to God. Sigh. Power Pusher, where is Bae?

Have You Considered

I listened to the sweetheart on the other end of the line very intensely. Nothing that she shared was new to my ears or thoughts. What I appreciated most was her honesty and awareness concerning how other believers treated her singleness. I could per-sonally relate. What I found to be interesting and alarming was her beautiful confidence in God that yielded her no fruit. She was void of manifestation in one major impactful area of her life, marriage. Her coaching call was not haphazardly scheduled out of crisis. It was based off of one premise and one prem-ise only, SOMETHING IS WRONG. She had taken the time to examine her life before making the call. She discerned what most didn't discern or cared to acknowledge, her problem was spiritual.

As I listened to the woman of God on the oth-er line speak, I heard a lot of self-examination. I heard a heart who understood that imperfections are not disqualifiers for love. I found her thoughts to-wards marriage to be balanced and positive. This woman of God had done her homework and her only resting conclusion was that something was wrong and that it was spiritual. I began to explore one as-pect of her life that I knew would hold clues to the chatter regarding her life in the realm of the spirit. I inquired about her dreams. Before I could clearly re-lease the word, dreams from out of my mouth, she resounded, "Yes, even my dreams testify that mar-riage is my portion. I often have dreams of getting married to a well-built man but I can never see his face. One time, we were about to get married but I couldn't find the wedding gown and he loving con-soled me. I've had dreams of my wedding ring. I saw the wedding ring on my finger several times and it was gorgeous, so I know that marriage is my portion. I'm ashamed to admit it but I've even had dreams of us having sex on the beach near our beach home. Power Pusher, we have a beach home so you know that Bae has money. Oh, I've had dreams of me giv-ing birth to our children; two girls and two boys. Like I said, I've never seen his face but God definite-ly showed me through my prophetic dreams that Bae is coming. Clearly his GPS is broken."

Lord have mercy was all that I could think as I buried my hands into my face while listening to this woman of God describe her dreams prophesying of her marital destiny. I couldn't help but wonder how she found my ministry but knew that it had to have been by the hand of God. Surely this woman knew (obviously not) that what she was describing were encounters with the incubus spirit. Surely someone taught her the signs and symptoms of an evil spir-itual marriage sponsored by the Marine Kingdom. I was both floored and disgusted by her spiritual bril-liance on one hand and complete ignorance on the other. For years, she had been walking around frus-trated and discouraged pertaining to marriage when her dreams held the foundational truth regarding why she discerned a cage around her marital destiny and an invisible cloak hiding her face from viable men. Sweet Jesus, how could I break it to this wom-an that based on what she disclosed, she will find it nearly impossible to break into a Kingdom marriage? My mind and heart were racing.

I confess that I was upset with her pastor and other spiritual teachers for not having such knowledge and teaching on it. They could have saved her much time and confusion. She could have longed warred herself into a place of freedom. I'm not sure how much time had gone by before being snatched back into awareness by the sound of my name being called. I'm assuming that I was silent long enough that the poor baby thought that I had disconnected from the line. I sluggishly reassured her that I was still there. Although, in that moment, I didn't want to be there anymore.

In my opinion, the call took a turn for the worst. I was bummed by what I heard because it meant tackling a very difficult topic. How would she accept what I needed to say and was she spiritually equipped for the fight for freedom that's ahead of her were some of my thoughts. I knew that she called for answers but I wasn't so sure if this particu-lar answer would sit well with her. Nevertheless, I was all in and reminded myself that I'm only the messenger. I'm not responsible for the reception. I cleared my throat and allowed truth to sing, "My dear, marriage is indeed your portion. You asked ear-lier, where's Bae? However, here's the problem, in the realm of the spirit, you already have a Bae and Bae is a demon."

The Punk Rock Millennial

Hello, are you there? Hello? Antoinette, are you there? This time, I was the one ensuring that the caller was still there. For what seemed like eternity, but was really long seconds, Antoinette's voice es-caped her and sound forsook my ears. After snap-ping her out of her silence, she stuttered, "I'm here." Relieved, I expressed that I was not in an environ-ment where I could go very deep but from every-thing that she shared with me, I was confident that my assessment was accurate. For years unbeknownst to her, she was fighting an incubus spirit designed to block her marital destiny. I apologized to her for the shock of hearing that she has a demonic Bae must have caused. More silence ensued that was soon vio-lated by tears. I felt her pain deep in my soul. She pushed her tears aside and communicated, "I need to call my pastor and get confirmation that my Bae is a demon before I receive anything more from you. I'll call you back when I'm done and let you know what he says."

Saints, you must understand that I am bold by nature so I knew that I needed to count to at least five before responding. I had to take into considera-tion that I had just dropped a major spiritual bomb on her. I'm accustomed to people coming to me for help because their spiritual leaders are not equipped to help them or they desire privacy. However, some-one saying to me that they needed to call their pastor for confirmation as to what God showed me was an absolute first and I was not willing to play the game. I could have understood if she said that she needed to disconnect in order to digest the news and pray but she didn't. If her pastor had the answers that she needed, God would not have directed her steps to me. He would have directed her steps to her pastor. Even so, I understood that more than likely she was groomed to seek her pastor's counsel and input in every aspect of her life; especially in spiritual cases. Sounds reasonable. However, did she ask her pas-tor's permission to call me or to repeat what he said in response to her inquiry regarding strengthening the singles in their church? I think not. Calling her pastor had nothing to do with the Holy Spirit but ra-ther, her spiritual pride. If anything, she should have been upset that the shepherd over her soul missed something so vital, she was in a demonic spiritual marriage.

I am pleased to share that I didn't lose my cool. I handled the situation like a saved and healed woman of God should have. I expressed that she was free to call her pastor and share everything that we discussed. However, I would not be there to answer her call once she was done. If your pastor whose leadership you've sat up under for years can sudden-ly confirm or deny the diagnosis to your problem, he can suddenly provide the solution. I thanked her for reaching out to me and encouraged her to research the subject matter further. She tried to keep the door of access open but my work was done. It was only a coaching call. Even so, I felt sad for her because she just didn't understand that no woman or man of God majors in everything and that's why there are different limbs on the body that performs different func-tions. This limb, had done its job. Even so, the knowledge of spiritual marriages should be in every single man or woman of God's tool box. Bishop T. D. Jakes taught me long ago that you can't save every-one and I believed him.

Preacher Lady

I packed my laptop, took my headphones off and placed them and my phone in my purse and was ready to roll out until I heard a mousy sounding voice whispering, "Excuse me, excuse me, Ms." I turned around and realized that it was the punk rock styled millennial who had been sitting next to me the entire time doing lord knows what. I noticed her because she was wearing all black and had several piercings and tattoos. More than anything else, I ob-served that she had the most beautiful pink Mo-hawk. What also stood out were her beautiful freck-les and almond shaped eyes that screamed, I'm a beautiful and innocent soul in need of guidance. Even so, I quickly dismissed her once I sat next to her because sounds of her horrific heavy metal music escaped her headphones and reminded me that Sa-tan is very much alive. Y'all, I'm not exaggerating. The music sounded so demonic that I wanted to move but had nowhere to go. I was stuck in town and needed to be sure that I was in place for the thir-ty minutes long coaching call. Any who, surprised by her desire to converse, I engaged. She preceded to speak the unexpected. "I overheard parts of your phone call. It's not like I was eavesdropping but my phone died and when I took my earphones off, I heard you mention the incubus spirit. Are you like a preacher lady or something? No disrespect. I'm not religious or anything. I don't really believe in God but I know that demon very well." I'm going to be honest, Readers, I didn't know what to say but I could discern the gift of the moment. I didn't need to say anything, just listen.

I sat back down and inquired if she was com-fortable chatting in such a public place and of course, the millennial with the pink hair was all in. So, I gave her a counselor's most favorite line, "Tell me more." Her dimples and eyes of promise peeking from beneath all of the piercings reminded me that I was talking to one of God's beautiful wayward ba-bies. That thought encouraged me to relax. I chose to see her as a sister and friend. She seemed pleased not to meet judgement from me. Addressing me more like one of her girlfriends who's capable of holding all of her secrets without spilling the beans, she gave me abrupt and brutal honesty that millen-nials are known for.

She Has A Demonic Bae

"Preacher lady, I have an incubus demon named, Roscoe and I want him gone but he won't go. My aunt is a witch and she told me that he was given to me in childhood. She suggested that he could offer me protection, comfort and promotion. She con-vinced me it would be a good idea to let him know that he is wanted in my life; especially since I was alone and having so many problems with men. Stu-pid I know but she is all the family that I have and I wanted to please her. I figured she knew best and assumed that if he was already there, why not em-brace him wholeheartedly. I ignorantly agreed to ex-plore the idea and I eventually went through the marital ritual to invoke him to be a part of my life full time. Preacher lady, I saw it enter the room and it addressed me by name. He told me about my en-tire life and how he loved and protected me. I'm talking about major secret things. He told me that he would protect and take care of me if I agreed to take him as my only lover. The sound of his voice made me feel cared for and the way that my life had been going, I had nothing to lose and I agreed.

"At first, it was fun and comforting until it wasn't. He comes and goes as he pleases. He does things to my body that I hate. It seems like every-thing in my life got worse with him around. I mean, I live well and my job is awesome but internally, I feel like an empty shell. I hate him and I'm desperate for him to leave. I'm probably in trouble for talking to you but you don't strike me as the scary type and I want to be like you. Preacher lady, I want him gone. I'm afraid to sleep at night because I know that he's coming. He even bothers me during the day. I rarely stay home so that I can keep busy and not have to deal with him pestering me on and off. I blast my music so that I can drown out his voice and my tor-menting thoughts. I told him that I don't want to be his wife anymore and he told me that he has rings on my fingers and that my soul belongs to him. Is that true? Am I tied to him for the rest of my life?"

There's A Way Out

Her inquisitive eyes glared into mine and I reassured her that there is definitely a way out but it's a pro-cess. And of course, the millennial blurted, "Do I have to become a Christian?" I answered as honestly as possible, "Well, you don't have to but it sure would be in your best interest." It was obvious that she was contemplating my answer. "Preacher lady, I know about Jesus. I like him but the truth is, He doesn't like me very much because I killed my father when I was fourteen. I decided that he was not going to rape me or beat my mother ever again. And so, I killed him and when I did, I lost both of my parents. My mother instantly hated me because I killed what she called, 'God's best gift to her.' Go figure. Years later, she went insane and killed herself. I can't re-member much about what happened next. All I know is that I spent years in juvie and then foster care before aging out. To my surprise, I got accepted into college and studied computer programming and I'm really good at it. That's how I make a living. I don't have a police or juvenile record and I don't ask why."

I found Samantha's story fascinating but not uncommon. I was eager to help but she needed to be prepped spiritually. For the next hour, I ministered to her through the power of the Holy Spirit and she accepted Christ as her personal savior. WHEW! God's power is amazing. Indeed it is but we were not done. She needed to be educated regarding spir-itual warfare and specifically, Roscoe and deliver-ance. I was not going to attempt deliverance prema-turely. She needed more understanding. And just when I thought that I could rest, her mousy-sounding voice perked up and she inquired, "I know how I got Roscoe, but how does a person usually contract or attract a spirit spouse? Is it a family thing because I swear that my whole family has one. We are pretty messed up. lol." I loved it whenever Sa-mantha smiled. Her smile was filled with the anoint-ing of God. I admired the way that God showed up in her smile.

Roscoe Manifests

I cleared my day because it now belonged to my new sister in Christ with the pink hair. I became even more relaxed and ordered a pizza because I was certain that we were going to be there for a while. It was fine by me. Talking to Samantha helped to dis-tract me from obsessing over Grier's situation.

Her flight to Nigeria was over thirteen hours long plus factoring in time for her to get acquainted with her future family. I reminded myself that God loves Grier more than I do and that it is his job to take care of her in ways that I could not. God did not call me to be what he already is to her, her protector. Pause. "WHAT?! Samantha, what's wrong? Samantha, are you ok?" Samantha looked at me with the most cyni-cal smile and released a grunt that sent chills up and down my spine. Oh well, looks like I'm meeting Ros-coe a lot sooner than I had anticipated. "Roscoe, in the name of Jesus, I bind you in chains and fetters. I strip you of your power. You will not harm this child of God anymore and at the appointed time, you will be permanently evicted from her body." Roscoe re-plied, "Preacher lady trying to take my wife. It ain't happening." I wanted to laugh but contained-my composure. His voice surprised me. He spoke with a slow country drawl. "Roscoe, once again, I bind you in the name of Jesus." Roscoe popped back, "Preach-er lady blind because I'm already bound. I'm not let-ting go, the covenant runs deep between us." This time, I smiled and commanded him to go back down and called Samantha back to the forefront. Samantha had no idea what transpired and I didn't tell her.

Study Your Opponent

In my much younger years, I was a cheerleader in middle and high school. I can remember one of our theme cheers, "Who you rooting for?" The middle school crowd would respond, "MMS." The initials stood for Manchester Middle School. In high school, the crowd roared, "FHS," representing, Furman High School. Those were the glory days of rocking the crowd and I miss them so much. Spiritually speaking, in order to effectively win the war of elim-inating your demonic Bae, you must be clear who's team you're on and what is being chanted regarding your life in the courts of heaven.

Imagine if you will, a band of angels chanting over your life as the father cries out, "Who you rooting for?!" And the angels all roar your initials. Yaaaaaas! Be very cognizant that the heavenly hosts are cheering and fighting with you as you engage your UNWANTED demonic Bae. I stressed unwanted because there are thousands upon thousands of people who enjoy and welcome their demonic Bae; Christians included. There are people who invoke said spirits because of the pleas-ure and pseudo comfort that they bring. Such people include the spiritually ignorant, workers of darkness, deeply wounded in their souls, and those who feel that God has forgotten about them and accepts that marriage is not their portion. Such persons have giv-en their souls over to their demonic Bae and they have no idea of the consequences. Perhaps you are one of those individuals who enjoys your demonic Bae's company because his visits feel good. No judgement. However, you need to make a decision today to reject him. Lift your hands wherever you are and pray, "In the name of Jesus, my demonic Bae cannot stay, I now declare him a stray!"

I mentioned earlier that I was a cheerleader in high school. Well, what I didn't mention is that my brothers were star football players. My brother Lou-is, number 88, played the position of middle line-backer. If he hit you on the field, trust me, you were not going to easily forget it. Players from across the region avoided number 88. His reputation preceded him. It was nothing for a hit from number 88 to send your helmet soaring across the field. I can still hear the pops that a tackle from my brother made and the oohh's and aahh's from the crowd. He could rock a crowd. The many newspaper articles and trophies combined from my brothers, Adrian, Frank, and Dar-ion made me and my parents very proud.

Cousin Louis

I recall one of my cousins from New York moving down south. During that time, it was a big deal liv-ing in the country and encountering a city kid. We were excited to welcome and embrace cousin Louis. However, there was a problem. He had a BIG MOUTH that rubbed some the wrong way. We made the mistake of taking him to one of our rival football games without first explaining to him the rules of engagement at a rivalry game. Sure enough, we beat the mess out of Maywood High. Without giving thought to cousin Louis' propensity to brag, after the school dance and while on the way to our cars to head home, a fight broke out, and guess who was at the center of the fight? You guessed it, cousin Louis.

This joker's New York accent captivated the women from both sides of the playing field. He drew a lot of attention and the country boys didn't like it. Howev-er, the boys from our side of the field ignored him because he was related to the DesChamps. We were a close community so we looked out for each other. To the boys from Maywood, he was too much. Not only did his New York swag irritate them, but his bragalicious-mouth taunting them about the beat down on the field set them all the way off. I had no idea of what was brewing.

Gleefully, I made it to the car with my then Bae. I was happy because the entire night was a success. That's until I looked up and saw that my brother Frank and cousin Louis were fighting. I later learned that my quiet and reserved brother jumped in to de-fend big-mouth cousin. I had never seen my brother fight before and I was afraid and amazed at the same time. He and cousin Louis were handling business until my then Bae decided to be a hero and insert himself into the fight. He opened the car door just as cousin Louis was making his way through the gang that was focused on him only to run straight into the door thusly knocking him down. The funniest but not so funny part of this story is that my then Bae decided to jump in the fight without counting the cost by sizing up his strength and boldness next to that of his opponents. He reacted without strategy.

Former Bae jumped in the fight, and to my ut-ter shock, one of the thugs reached out and slapped the taste from out of his mouth. Lawwwwwd! Read-ers, excuse me for a moment. Samantha is laughing uncontrollably and now I'm giggling too. Whew, ok, I'm back! Before I knew it, I was consoling Bae's pride and trying to gather what led to the altercation. I know that this story is funny and you're probably thinking that I should have celebrated him for at least trying. Possibly but please understand, I am a country girl and country girls take pride in having a strong man who can throw down if need be. All that I can remember is Bae getting slapped and rubbing his face. SMH! He greatly overestimated himself and underestimated his opponent. Y'all, Samantha is still laughing. SMH!

Power, Confidence, Strategy & Authority

Let me go ahead and bring this on home before I lose Samantha to the spirit of laughter. In the realm of the spirit, you want to be like my brother Frank and develop a name for yourself by the power that you exude. This power is built through prayer, bible study, and developing a consistent, intimate rela-tionship with God. Demons should fear your connec-tion with God. Cousin Louis represents the unique-ness and confidence that you should walk with. A confidence that irritates hell and inspires those who aren't familiar with Kingdom confidence and author-ity. My former Bae represents your willingness and eagerness to fight without first assessing and gather-ing strategy.

Reader, you may be living on earth, but you must tap into your residence of origin, and that's heaven. Your heritage and residency entitles you to benefits, and one of those benefits is authority backed by God. Your authority is foreign to the in-habitants of this land who are not connected to your place of origin. However, your authority is not for-eign or underestimated to the inhabitants of dark-ness. Their desire is that you never understand nor operate in your authority given by God.

You are a part of a family of winners and your last name is Kingdom. In your case, like cousin Lou-is, you can brag and run your mouth once you learn and understand the rules of engagement because then and only then will you be equipped to fight and win when the clap back comes. Although I'm speak-ing spiritually, you can't do like my former Bae did in the natural. Although well-meaning, you can't jump into this spiritual fight unequipped and ill-prepared. This is done by trying to counsel and de-liver others and yourself while unequipped to exe-cute a win because you didn't wisely educate your-self regarding your opponent. Don't just open the door and jump in the fight. Prepare!

STUDY

BEFORE you venture into fighting your demonic Bae and his relatives, demanding that power change hands, it is ESSENTIAL that you first study Bae and your demonic in-laws. Learning as much as you can about your opponent will better position you to re-gain your territory and position in the least amount of time while exerting the least amount of energy. So relax. Don't rush through this book. Let every word, every chapter, every concept, sizzle in your spirit!

Barshook

Without realizing it, my body language shifted and Samantha caught it. My mind briefly wandered back to Grier and our spiritual warfare boot camp ses-sions. Just like Samantha, she was eager to learn about demonic Baes. However, unlike Samantha, her demonic Bae was not hers. The demonic Bae stalking her belonged to Guvnah. He's ancestral and his name is Barshook. I guess this is a sound place to share with you why I'm concerned about Grier. I don't want to present as the codependent friend with unnatural affections. I am a spiritual warfare tactical specialist. This is what God called me to do so anything spiritual warfare laced piques my inter-est.

So, let me bring you and Samantha up to speed. Barshook confronted Grier three separate times. The first time was in a dream on the night that Guvnah professed his love for her. Barshook showed up and communicated that he was the family idol and he was assigned to Guvnah to ensure that he rose in life and to offer him protection. In order to continue receiving his love, she must also profess her allegiance to him or she would be removed from his life. He warned her to stop filling his head with Christian rhetoric because great plans had already been made for his life. Barshook ended the conversa-tion by stating that Grier and her destiny was con-cerning enough for him to kill her on the spot. Ac-cording to Grier, when he threatened her life, the wind of God engulfed her. She looked Barshook straight in the eyes and stated, "My life belongs to the Most High God. To touch me is to touch fire. In the name of Jesus, I command you to flee." And that he did.

Samantha was intrigued. "Preacher lady, did she tell Guvnah? What did he say?" "Yes, she told him and he was shook. He confirmed that their fami-ly idol is named Barshook. He believed Grier because there was no way that she could have known all that she did. That was the day that

Guvnah gave his heart to Christ and renounced the witchcraft of his family. He stated that everyone in the village and family fears Barshook. They nicknamed him Lord of Death because when crossed, even over the most minute thing, death becomes your portion. The mere fact that Grier stood up to him and lived to tell about it convicted Guvnah of the hierarchy and sovereignty of the Christian's God."

Samantha's Deliverance

I was stunned by Samantha's reaction to what I was sharing with her. She was crying and slowly her hands began to ascend into the posture of worship and she began praying to the sovereign God of the universe. She didn't care where she was or who was watching. She was having a sincere and unprovoked worship experience. And to my utter amazement, my pink-haired sister with the tattoos and piercings uttered with boldness and authority, "God, I'm sorry that me and my ancestors invited Roscoe into our lives. It is in your name only that he will leave. I don't want him in my life. Roscoe, I am not afraid of you anymore. You are not greater than Jesus. So I'm telling you now to leave my body and life forever."

Reader, without being prompted or coached, Samantha grabbed the to-go bag from the table and filled it with demonic debris. When she was done, she calmly discarded the bag, walked to the bath-room, rinsed her mouth out, and washed her face. I looked around and no one was paying us any atten-tion. Everyone was preoccupied. I just sat in awe of God's timing. A simple story led to her deliverance from Roscoe. Only God!

When Samantha reentered the room, she was glowing with God's glory. She sat down and looked me straight in the eyes and said, "preacher lady, I'm free. Please teach me what you know so that I can grow and help others like myself." My God from Zi-on what a divine setup! "Samantha, it would be my absolute pleasure." My eager student pulled out a brand new red notebook as if she prophetically saw this moment coming. It is said, when the student is ready, the teacher will appear.

What We Know

The Kingdoms of darkness are vast and mysterious. What we as deliverance ministers have come to un-derstand extends from a culmination of studying the word of God, revelation from God, insight from for-mer agents of darkness, personal experience, and rhetoric from demons on their way out of a body. I will share with you what we know about demonic Baes, but only what's relevant to your freedom. There is much to learn and explore. With that being said, I don't believe for a moment that God desires for his children to major in the ins and outs of dark-ness. That's dangerous territory and many have lost their way by delving too deep in spiritual warfare. Years ago, I distanced myself from a deliverance minister who enjoyed talking to demons too much for my comfort. During her sessions, she spent much time talking to them in an attempt to fish for hidden ancient secrets, information concerning herself, and bloodlines. Her methods made me feel very uncom-fortable.

Yes, we should learn as much as possible about our opponent, but our untamed curiosity can risk leading into dangerous territory. With that being said, I do believe that some of us are called, guided, and protected to go a little deeper than the average. However, there is a difference in knowing that de-mons rape humans versus inquiring if it feels good to them, what positions they prefer, and what types of humans they desire. None of that information is spiritually profitable nor aides in freeing men and women of God from bondage.

My Personal Belief

When I compile all of the natural and spiritual knowledge that I've accumulated over the years, there is no doubt in my mind that the majority of the population has a demonic Bae and that's one of the main reasons why relationships bring so many mys-terious complications. Relationship experts are abso-lutely wonderful but often fall short by alleviating the importance of establishing a solid spiritual foun-dation. And those who do value and promote build-ing spiritually sound foundations, downplay or ig-nore the role the demonic plays in fighting relation-ships. Therefore, a beautiful couple with much promise and potential, when under attack, can pre-sent as a couple from hell. When in actuality, they aren't a couple from hell, but they are a couple haunted by hell. Without spiritual insight, emotional and sometimes physical damage is done that leads to a needless divorce or breakup. At the core, these couples love each other and are internally confused as to WHY they can't mesh. They have no revelation why their romantic connections are such a struggle. Consider what Barshook said to Grier. He told her that he had the power to remove her from Guvnah's life. Ponder how he could accomplish such.

There are so many valid theories and statistics attempting to explain why, but they are in most cas-es, symptoms but not the foundational causes for re-lational enmity. The least explored factor to be con-sidered is the reality that hosts of unsuspecting men and women are involved in Spiritual Sex Trafficking that labels their marital status as taken in the realm of the spirit. Pulling directly from chapter 11 in my first book, You Already Know ... You Can't Build On A Demonic Foundation, Spiritual Sex Trafficking is a term that I coined in my pursuit to describe the in-voluntary sexual hijacking of a person by demons in the spirit realm. These demons not only violate them sexually, but they also go as far as claiming the per-son as their spouse or lover. These entities turn their chosen Baes into their spiritual sex slaves.

The Marine Kingdom

Demonic Baes can be referred to as, spirit spouses, spirit husbands, or spirit wives. They take their or-ders from their governing demons, Incubus and Suc-cubus. In Latin, Incubus means to lie upon and Suc-cubus means to lie under. Incubus is the demon that descends upon the female and Succubus is the de-mon that descends upon the male. Incubus and Suc-cubus are what we call, Marine Kingdom demons, better known as water spirits. Some clans of demons and fallen angels who live in various bodies of water all across the world make up the Marine Kingdom .

The Marine Kingdom is a spiritual kingdom that can be accessed through the spirit realm. There are other demonic kingdoms such as forest, moun-tains, hell, and solar. However, Marine Kingdom demons are believed to be the most powerful of all the demonic kingdoms because they specialize in se-duction and all that feeds man's vanity addiction. Their headquarters is in the Indian Ocean governed by the demon, Queen of India. The Queen Of The Coast is her boss and she governs the Atlantic seas. The Marine Kingdom is known for their influence over cosmetics, storms, pharmaceuticals, street drugs, eccentric hairstyles, weave, fashion, politics, technology, perfumes, and ALL things dealing with sexual lust and perversion. They are some of the most violent, vicious, meanest, and down-right wicked demons in the game.

Marine king demons specialize in seducing and baiting humanity into sexual defilement. All sexual dreams, sex addictions, and sexual violations are directly or indirectly sponsored by them. The downfall of the prominent to the least is more than likely sponsored by their kingdom. They are very jealous, possessive, and patient in their quest to con-quer. Some of the popular demons from their un-derwater kingdom include Jezebel, python, incubus and succubus, leviathan, queen of the coast, queen of India, Asmodee, Asmodai, and the mermaid spirit called, Mami Wata. Of course the list goes on and on!

Their Origin & Mission

Many credible Bible scholars agree that the sons of God were indeed angels on assignment in the earth realm who decided to forsake their assignment. A few commentators that I read argued that the scrip-ture is referring to the descendants of Cain and Able joining together in marriage. However, the usage of the Hebrew term, "sons of God," appears in the Old Testament over four times, and the definition found in Gen 6:2 is the same meaning that's found in Job 38:4 when describing the angels of God shouting for joy. Daniel 3:24-25 and Job 1:6 support the same. So yes, these were angels of God who walked out of re-lationship and grace. WOW and WOW! These trai-tors ventured to marry the beautiful daughters of men. It's not that they were in love because darkness doesn't know love. Rather, they were in lust. When they aborted their assignment, as free agents, they were turned over to darkness.

"And the angels which kept not their first estate, but left their own habitation, he hath reserved in ever-lasting chains under darkness unto the judgment of the great day." Jude 1:6

These angels did not rebel with Lucifer and his posse. They later rebelled. My God! I believe that as they were going to and fro, running errands for God, they entertained conversations with some of their old angel friends and as a result, they became tempted and enticed to abort home. Perhaps their friends accused God to them and played on some seeds of uncertainty that were planted while Lucifer was recruiting for his rebellion initiative. Perhaps watching their friends get kicked out of heaven con-fused them. Who knows for sure but the rebellious ones and God. All that we know is that they rebelled and started lusting after God's daughters and crossed the supernatural lines by having sex with the daughters of God as eluded to in Jude 1:7.

"Even as Sodom and Gomorrah, and the cities about them in like manner, giving themselves over to forni-cation, and going after strange flesh, are set forth for an example, suffering the vengeance of eternal fire."

As if sin wasn't enough, they further diluted and polluted the bloodline's/DNA of the women they married. Children were born to these unions. And as a result, the Nephilim race was created. A Nephilim is a half-human, half-spirit being. The way that they were able to reproduce is tied to very dark works of evil and that is why their offspring were birthed with supernatural powers.

These rebellious angels, once outside of God's counsel, made it their mission to instruct humanity how to tap into the supernatural outside of God. Think of it this way, they taught humanity how to break into cars and hot wire them versus legally ob-taining permission and gaining access utilizing the correct methods, keys and permission. They were the FIRST to push the WOKE agenda. They were the FIRST to instruct humanity regarding their third eye. Earth's first occultists, spiritualists, witches, and warlocks were trained and established by fallen an-gels. They pushed a polytheistic society. Among oth-er dark acts, they taught humanity the mysteries that are embedded in the elements of the earth, including the solar system. Because they are void of light, they pervert everything that they touch, just like their adopted daddy, Satan. Keep in mind, as you pursue your freedom, Satan is not equal to God. He is noth-ing more than a highly intelligent and very powerful fallen angel. Even so, his intelligence and power be-longs to God. The same God who gave you authority over him in Luke 10:19.

The Displaced Ones

We have already established that a Nephilim is a half-breed supernatural human. Prior to the flood, the word of God tells us that humanity was out of control. Things were so bad that every imagination and thought of man was evil (Gen 6:5). Thankfully, God found a family who honored him and he asked the patriarch, Noah, to build an Ark in preparation for the catastrophic flood that he was sending to cleanse the earth. Everything not on the ark, at the appointed time, would die (Gen 6:7-9). As you may well know, spirits cannot die. Therefore, their hu-man bodies were destroyed during the flood but their spirits were not. As a result, they became dis-embodied spirits.

I am one who subscribes to the thought that demons are different from fallen angels. I along with other Bible scholars believe that demons are actually the disembodied Nephilim spirits from the flood. There is the Incubus, Succubus sect that specializes in continuing the perverted practices of "marrying" humans that was first introduced by their ancestors. They seek men and women whom they can attach to spiritually and claim as their bride or groom. These spirits are trying to counterfeit an institution that does not belong to them, marriage. And yes, in the realm of the spirit, they are able to procreate with the subjects of their affection thusly producing what is known as, spirit children; spawns of Satan. I have watched many spirit children manifest during deliverance sessions. I've even witnessed spirit spouses crying or becoming enraged over their deaths.

Do Demons Have Sexual Organs?

When I first started learning this information, I was intrigued and confused at the same time. One of my questions was, do angels have sex organs? The thought perplexed my mind. Although I cannot an-swer that question with certainty, and neither can anyone else, let's consider that we are talking about the spirit realm. The realm that we know very little about besides it's the unseen realm where anything is possible. The Bible warns us that fallen angels can transform into whatever form they desire, including angels of light (2 Corinthians 11:14). Therefore, spir-itual logic calculates that they can manifest sexual organs if need be. Demonic Baes can operate with an hermaphrodite ability. They can manifest both sex organs. Depending upon the assignment, they can manifest female on female and/or male on male. This usually occurs when they want to initiate a per-son into homosexuality or lesbianism or to deepen the tie.

What we do know for sure is that demonic Baes have sex with the person in their dreams, while they are wide awake, or while they are drifting into a dreamlike state. They rarely show up as themselves, but rather as someone you're familiar or unfamiliar with, and in most cases, fits the type of person you would be attracted to in the natural. Samantha's mouth was wide open. Trust me, my mind was too when I first started learning this information.

Do Demons or Fallen Angels Marry?

Readers, another question that harassed my mind was, do demons or angels marry? If we were to con-sider this question from a scriptural point of view, I would have to conclude that angels of God do not marry nor, to the best of my knowledge, do they re-produce (Matthew 22:30). However, we are talking about fallen angels and demons. They are counter-feiters and whatever those jokers put their hands on, they defile. Remember, when I refer to demonic Baes marrying humans, it's a spiritual marriage with the sole purpose to defile God's creation and to mimic Holy institutions established by God.

Keep in mind, Fallen angels and demons have distinct personalities and they judge beauty as indi-cated in the Bible:

When human beings began to increase in number on the earth and daughters were born to them, the sons of God saw that the daughters of humans were beau-tiful, and they married any of them they chose… The Nephilim were on the earth in those days — and also afterward — when the sons of God went to the daugh-ters of humans and had children by them. They were the heroes of old, men of renown. Genesis 6:1-2, 4 (NIV)

Demons have personalities. They can be at-tracted to certain things about you. It's nothing for them to compliment their host's body parts and per-sonality during deliverance. Samantha interjected, "Preacher lady, so much is making sense. Roscoe used to compliment me a lot. It was creepy but I liked it because it was attention. He told me that he was from the water but I declined to inquire what he meant." "Once when I told him that I wanted him to leave me alone, he stated that I was ignorant and ungrateful. Apparently men and women engage his kingdom for riches, protection, and influence. He said that I would be surprised how many of the world's favorite politicians, spiritual influencers, and stars beseech his kingdom for permission to capti-vate and influence people like myself. He bragged that anybody who's anybody came to his kingdom for blessings to rise. With him in my life, I could turn the unfavorable in my favor if I played my cards right. He boasted that I could take spots that I didn't qualify for and achieve what would otherwise be de-nied unto me." So much of what she stated con-firmed what I taught about demons. Intrigued, I in-quired how did she resist engaging for power? Her response led me to believe that God was with her for sure. "Preacher lady, his offers didn't excite me be-cause I'm a minimalist. All I really desired was love and I foolishly thought that he could give it to me because I had nothing to compare it to. Sadly, I can understand how appealing the dark world can be-come to those who are desperate, seeking fame, and are looking for fortune and have lost their way. Preacher lady, I understand how we benefit, but how do they? What's in it for them? What does Satan want?" Intrigued by her question I was, "Samantha, excellent question!"

What Satan Wants

Samantha's question was loaded and I had answers. Satan wants to be worshipped and revered. Satan knows that most people, Christian or not, would not knowingly enter into a covenant with a dark entity with their end result leading to doom. The infallible word of God instructs us not to be ignorant of his devices (2 Corinthians 2:11). He has many ways of ensnaring humanity. My goal is to expose his device of spiritual marriages.

Satan highjacks and forges spiritual marriages/covenants with people without their consent or through their spiritual ignorance and the holes in their soul. Even if you are trying to live right in the natural, your demonic Bae strategically plots to ruin your reputation in the realm of the spirit so that he can have an excuse to accuse you before God. Once Satan or one of his cohorts claims a person, they taint God's glory and likeness in them and frustrate their godly inheritance.

Spiritual Defilement

By now, I am sure that you get the point that it's not about sexual pleasure for the kingdom of darkness. It's about spiritual defilement. Every time that de-monic Bae violates you sexually, he is defiling you spiritually. Every time that demonic Bae hits it, he's depositing something into you and taking something away from you. Let me make it even clearer, when he's sexually violating you or pinning you down (you call it the hag), that's when he deposits: moni-toring devices, demonic triggers, special opts de-mons, evil charms, evil subliminal messages, demon-ic codes, and mind control devices. These are im-planted specifically to manipulate and control you.

This is so dangerous because it's demonic Bae who holds the remote. They can also mark you and/or put evil scents on you that attract scenarios that keep you in distress versus in a position of rest. Scenarios such as premature death, chronic acci-dents, poverty, barrenness, regression, delay, and rejection don't even scratch the surface regarding what these powers are capable of. This is how such problems become cyclical. You're demonically pro-grammed. This is also how a child of the King's life can look completely jacked up. Because Satan is the creator of nothing good or original, he takes the good virtues that he steals and gives them to his workers of iniquity. And this is how it can seem that some sinners are prospering over blood-bought believers.

Samantha interjected with a hardy, "Amen." She recounted that even though she wasn't a believ-er at the time, her life began to take a downward spi-ral upon aggressively embracing Roscoe. She became dark in appearance which attracted more rejection into her life. For what seemed like no justifiable rea-son, she got demoted at work. Looking back, the re-jection and demotion were reactionary responses. Ignorant to the cause, that's when she started rebel-ling against society and started wearing all black, ex-cessively tattooing and piercing her body, and invit-ing heightened sexual deviance between her and Roscoe. She articulated that her taste in music and movies became ashamedly dark. Roscoe encouraged her to embrace the new her because it was the true her, and she believed him.

Seeds of Perversion

Demons need a place of habitation to freely move about the earth and your body provides that. Until evicted, they will use your body as a base of opera-tion to carry out their dirty deeds. In the case of de-monic Baes, they desire to plant seeds of perversion that will take root in your mind, body, will, and emo-tions that causes you to take on their lustful and per-verted characteristics.

This brand of demon desires that you derail yourself and hopefully infect those that you come into contact with. For example, a perverted father will encourage perversion in his sons. He will find manly humor and pride in knowing that his sons are masturbating to porn, and/or having premarital sex. The mother who's filled with bitterness and disappointment sponsored by her demonic Bae, will see no issue with encouraging her daughters to disre-spect men and use them for money. An aunt who's filled with lust will teach her nieces how to catch and keep a man using their bodies. The pastor who's perverted will sleep with his members even if blow-ing his witness is the price to be paid. The porn-addicted man will risk losing his job and home in quest of his next sexual high. The music producer with a demonic Bae will ensure that his artists are highly sensual and make music that promotes the opposite of sexual purity.

Our Nation

A nation filled with citizens with demonic Baes will use abortion as birth control, sex appeal will be used to promote almost everything, fornication will be the norm, the LGBT community will be able to intimi-date believers into silence for fear of being canceled, porn will be a 90 billion dollar industry, sex traffick-ing won't be aggressively attacked, child sex abuse rates will continue rising, calling women bitches and whores will be acceptable, and preachers of the gos-pel will proudly marry worldly women who take no issue with half dressing while disrespecting the god-ly standard of modesty while striking out against those who speak up; all without losing members.

You're A Believer

You say that you are a believer so let's talk! Your demonic Bae understands what you do not, when you are defiled spiritually, you stand tainted in the eyes of God. When you are defiled, agents of dark-ness can rightfully build an accusatory case against you in heaven, thus blocking your blessings from freely traveling to you on earth and that includes your marital destiny. Take this fight seriously. They are stubborn and are not to be played with and de-pending upon the complexity of your foundation and type, they can be HELL to evict.

You have sized up your opponent and you're either intimidated or ready to rumble. Prayerfully, the latter, because no matter how powerful this kingdom, glory to the Most High God, your demonic Bae and his family can be shut down! Power MUST change hands, and you have the authority to make it so. One last thing, oftentimes, we get so wrapped up in the benefits that ridding your life of these spirits can bring. Let's remember that sexual sin is sin. Therefore, be very mindful that getting set free from your demonic Bae will also affect where you spend all of eternity.

The Text

"Preacher lady, this is what I don't get. This infor-mation is so straightforward. Why aren't more Christians teaching this? It was easy for Roscoe to leave my body. What's the problem?" "Samantha, I hear you and I'm not sure why God came for you to-day. I'm glad that he did. Maybe it's your childlike faith that moved God. You didn't come as a know it all, ashamed of your condition or sin, you admitted your wrong and wanted to correct it. Samantha are you listening? Put your phone down. Samantha what's wrong?"

Sam, I know what you did to Roscoe and I'm not happy. I stuck my neck out for you and you betrayed me. I have to pay for your actions and that's not cool. It's not going to fly. You best believe that we are coming for you. To make things easier on us both, renounce what you did, and let's talk ASAP or conse-quences will follow.

That's the text that Samantha's aunt who in-ducted her into witchcraft sent. It shook her because according to her, auntie is a high-ranked witch. Sigh. It's so like the enemy to refuse to let go without a fight. This is a form of backlash. I talked Samantha back into a place of confidence, but secretly, I was concerned. Her aunt meant business and I knew it. What I needed to do was to ensure that we closed all doors by thoroughly praying various prayers of re-nunciation. I also knew that this meant that I needed to visit her home and anoint it. Going alone was out of the question and also unprofessional, so after ex-plaining the process to Samantha and getting her permission, I solicited the help of my assistant and prayer warrior, Opal. I filled her in as best as possi-ble before asking her to swing by my house and pick up my dog

Scout then meet me at Samantha's house. I knew that she would round up our deliverance crew so I drew confidence in knowing that I had help coming.

I asked Samantha to make a list of everything that her aunt had ever given her and any and every-thing in her home that she used to practice witch-craft and/or bought from witchcraft-type venues. Sheesh, I didn't expect her list to be so long. Oh my God! Jesus, she's on her second page, and from the looks of things, she's not slowing down any time soon. So, I'll use this time to talk to those of you who are believers and know that you have a demonic Bae. I would like to know what's taken you so long to get serious about divorcing and evicting your demonic Bae? Even at this point, are you equipped?

You Ain't Ready

I am a descendant of slaves and when I meditate on the spiritual implications of sex trafficking, and where God fits into the narrative, my mind travels to my slave ancestors whose marital beds were defiled by their evil slave masters. When slave men jumped over the broom with the Bae of their affection or the Bae chosen for them, they knew that it was highly probable that their union would later be tarnished by their slave owner or anyone closely associated with him. The risk of their Bae being raped or mishandled could quickly become his worst nightmare made a reality. History supports that vile slave owners felt they had a legal right to dehumanized the negro and saw them as nothing more than property. They showed no sanctity for the descendants of Africa. Displaying disrespect to their marital covenants was a walk in the park. Slave women were the slave owner's property, so what were their husbands to do during the occurrences of disrespect? At most, they were provoked to jealousy, anger and hate. These beautiful men whose skin had been kissed by the sun had authority but no power to use it. Talking about psychological emasculation at its finest! They watched helplessly and in humiliation as their beau-tiful Baes were disrespected and violated repeatedly at the master's choosing. I'm sure that some tried to fight but were quickly enlightened to their power-lessness.

Similarly, this is what our Father experiences when he watches His Bae, the church (2 Corinthians 11:2) being raped and molested by demons. He is in-deed provoked to jealousy because unlike the slaves, we are free. What can be done when his bride refus-es to play her part to break free and choose Him and only Him? Demonic Baes don't care about your Christian title, if you're espoused to someone else, or what your heart desires. In demonic Bae's eyes, you are its husband/wife. You are its property and slave. Demonic Bae is quite aware of God's presence in your life but he knows there are spiritual laws that govern the kingdoms of light and darkness. And when any of those laws are violated, oh legalistic slew foot Satan and his minions take accusations against a person to God as justification to steal, kill, and destroy. Repeat offenders tie God's sovereign hands because in most cases, the claims of demonic attacks and spiritual bondage are justifiable accord-ing to the works of your hands or someone in your bloodline.

Are You Equipped

The story doesn't stop here. There is a way of escape, a way out, if you please. God is waiting for your par-ticipation in repentance and the determination to take by force your emancipation from your demonic Bae. God does very little in the earth realm without invitation. That's why holiness and prayer are essen-tial and are your lifelines to freedom. You cannot win high-level spiritual wars without understanding how to activate and launch your authority and pow-er over the enemy. And let me tell you, permanently shutting down your demon Bae is a high-level battle. Without including the world in the equation, the ma-jority of believers are not equipped to engage in spir-itual warfare for the following reasons.

A lack of knowledge

Spiritually dumb is a term that sounds very harsh but accurately describes the overall state of the Christian church. So many profess to believe but don't understand the basic fundamental beliefs of their chosen religion. That my friends is unaccepta-ble. This is why the church as a whole has an identi-ty problem and its participants are so welcoming to all winds of belief. This is also why doctrines of dev-ils can easily penetrate the minds of God's children. Bible study and prayer are being neglected. This generation seeks the hand of God without knowing God. The church is struggling with foundational bib-lical knowledge and is barely staying afloat; no won-der why so many roll their eyes at spiritual warfare. It's impossible to effectively engage in spiritual war-fare without a solid biblical foundation. Not much will make sense to you. A lot of the supernatural concepts will seem like exaggerated stories or flat-out lies. And as a result, the knowledge that you are exposed to will sit on the surface of your heart; ex-posed and easily accessible for the ravens to con-sume.

Biblical Foundation

If you cannot articulate how the war between good and evil began and what Jesus' death, burial, and resurrection symbolizes, you ain't ready to engage the enemy. If you cannot articulate what Jesus' death, burial, and resurrection gave you in terms of authority, you ain't ready to engage in spiritual war-fare. If you cannot name at least ten weapons of war-fare, you are ain't ready to war. If you cannot verbal-ly resist the devil and articulate hot fire prayers, you ain't ready. Lastly, you must be able, to the best of your ability, pinpoint the areas where the enemy is stealing, killing, and destroying in your life. In a pre-vious chapter, we discussed the importance of ad-mitting our truth so that we can be helped. So wher-ever you are, raise your hands and ask the Lord to equip you so that you can become battle-ready. Ask Him to do a QUICK work in you! I encourage you to stop what you're doing and go to Amazon and order my book on Spiritual warfare. In it, I cover the need to knows regarding spiritual warfare. Get your bible and reference every scripture mentioned. Sweetie, don't rush through building your foundation. With prayer and supplication, make your requests known unto God. I'm excited for you because your perishing days are about to be over.

Spiritually Distracted

This one is a biggie. Sometimes a person has enough knowledge to break free but they lack the fortitude and discipline required. They have not learned to bring their time and focus under the subjection of the Holy Spirit. They give their best to the workforce while leaving home neglected. Amazingly, many of them are active in church making their pastor's vi-sion a reality while suffering spiritually. Even so, their free time is eaten up by social media, television, and other sources of entertainment. The Holy Spirit further showed me that there are many whose time is consumed by the busyness of trying to appease their children by putting them in every activity pos-sible. They don't understand that God is intentional and not the God of busyness.

It's hard to hear God in the midst of the noise. It usually takes a crisis to get their attention and they war for breakthrough versus the eradication of the sender. When they find a good spiritual rhythm, the enemy throws relief in order to tame their hot fire prayers. He seduces them into thinking that they are free when in all actuality, they are not. He ensures that he sends a distraction that will eat up their time and attention until he strikes again. For many, the distraction is usually a relationship. The enemy will continue to have the upper hand until such persons understand that they should play this spiritual game of life from an offensive position versus a defensive position.

It's wise to wake up every morning and give God praise and the devil and his network a black eye. In order to overcome, you must be vigilant, dis-ciplined, and strategic. If you can't get around your busy schedule, wake up earlier. Leave the workplace chatter and turn your break time into your worship time. Turn off Ricky Smiley and Tom Joyner. Utilize your drive or ride to work as a time to seek God for yourself. If you ride with someone, inform them that you will no longer be a part of the profitless chatter. Put on your headphones and listen to what will build your spirit. Discipline your children not to in-terrupt you under any circumstances when you are seeking God. Be creative by putting a sign on the door alerting them that you are with God and that time is not to be interrupted. They will later mirror your actions. Try taking every other Saturday or Sunday off from corporate worship and spend the day in God's presence. Develop a set time to meet with God that no one can interrupt. You have more time to seek God than you think. Take authority over the darts of distraction. Don't make it easy for the enemy to capture you.

Personal Open Doors

It is not strange for some Christians to shy away from engaging in spiritual warfare because they do not want to walk away from their sin of choice. They usually say things like, "Spiritual warfare is not to be played with and I know that my life isn't right. I'm not going to engage until I'm ready; I respect God too much." Rubbish. If they truly had respect for God, they would abort the sin in their life and pursue freedom. What they truly mean is that they enjoy their demon of choice and they know better than to front on the demon that they have embraced because there will be serious consequences. They fear the wrath of demons over the wrath of God. And they also foolishly believe that tomorrow is always prom-ised. Kobe Bryant's death and the coronavirus has shown us that it is not.

Spiritual Pride

This is an area that I encounter quite often in spiritu-al leaders. They'd rather suffer than admit that they are in need of deliverance. They somehow believe that to admit that they are undone is weakness or beneath them. Obviously, they don't understand that even physicians find themselves in need of a physi-cian from time to time. Deliverance ministers need ministering to just like everyone else. I know this from experience. Ministers are human vessels with spiritual deficits just like errrrbody else. I sometimes have to wrestle with the ones that do come to be ministered to because their spiritual pride drives them to attempt to showboat how much they know about spiritual warfare. It takes much wrestling to get such persons to calm down and submit to the process. Even so, I give them major props for com-ing. It's the ones who make a lot of spiritual noise but aren't free that stress my Holy Ghost the most. They are filled with knowledge and can be found on every deliverance page possible. However, their bragging is bottom shelf because they have no idea how to piece together all of the information that they have for the profitable gain of freedom. Their spir-itual pride prevents them from humbling themselves and asking for help in order to devise a tailor-made way of escape from the tempter's snare.

Leaders Blocking

And then there are those who believe in deliverance but their understanding is surface understanding. They mislead God's people into believing that they are being delivered when in actuality, they are being deceived. And when someone who truly knows what they are doing comes to town, they release a controlling sound of sabotage that intimidates their members from supporting. I remember administer-ing deliverance in one of the Carolina's and the visit-ing prophet removed all of his members while I was ministering. I felt so sad for his congregants because they were being convicted as they listened to me minister. However, I could see their prophet mani-festing spiritual pride to the point that he couldn't take it anymore and interrupted the flow. Even so, they are still better and higher than the clergyman who unashamedly preach that deliverance isn't rele-vant to today's church. They walk with much spir-itual pride and it does so much harm in the lives of their followers who truly need it.

He's Sizing You Up

Just like you're sizing him up, he's sizing you up too. The enemy knows who's qualified to battle him ver-sus who isn't. If you fall into any of the above cate-gories, you have a decision to make. The battle that you are about to fight requires preparation, focus, and patience. I can't stress enough that this is not going to be a quick war. You are not going to win this fight overnight. I am going to tell you right now that shouting, speaking in tongues, praying, and fasting are great but are not enough to break free and stay free. To win the fight against your demonic Bae, you have to intelligently dismantle his kingdom by attacking him at the altar of its conception. And part of that entails finding your hand in your bondage and removing it.

In addition, the charge against you may have nothing to do with you but everything to do with who you're related to. My God! It's time to bring his kingdom to an end in your life and on behalf of the bloodline. Deep breath. No worries. No fear. By the time you are done with this two-part series, you will have a clear understanding of how to accomplish such. What is certain, it's time to put an end to de-mons laughing and winking at your creator and si-lencing your prayers all because they know the pain-ful truth; you are unqualified to be rescued because you are spiritually unequipped. It's time to further explore what gives demon Baes the legal right to claim you as their Bae. Yaaaaaaaas, it's about to go down. Knowledge is power! And utilized power equals FREEDOM! Raise your hands and tell the Lord thank you. However, before we go there, let's pause long enough to cleanse Samantha's house.

The Process of Deliverance

The drive from the cafe to Samantha's house was seven minutes walking distance and thanks to traf-fic, twenty minutes by car. Samantha walked to the cafe so I invited her to ride with me to her house. Opal sent me a text alerting me that she was at Sa-mantha's house already. It just so happened that she was in her neighborhood looking at houses. Know-ing her, she was sitting in her car meditating or walking around the premises praying.

Samantha tried to strike up a conversation, but I politely informed her that I was in prayer mode and encouraged her to pray too. She inquired what should she say. I didn't have time to do a lot of instructing so I encouraged her to focus on the list that she made and where to discard the witchcraft paraphernalia. I also instructed her to pray repeatedly, *I cover myself in the sacrificial blood of Jesus Christ. I choose him as my Savior, therefore, no weapons aimed at me shall prosper. Ho-ly Ghost fire over me and all that's attached to me.*

The closer that we got to the house, the more my stomach and back began to alarm me that war-fare was near. I kept driving and praying. I tried hard to keep my mind on God and what was ahead. The cars honking and Samantha's fidgety behavior com-peted for my attention. I glanced over and realized that Samantha was slightly manifesting. I expected this but not so soon. She was deeply involved in the occult and there's no telling how many demons are housed in her body. To make matters worse, over the sound of my bossy GPS personally barking direc-tional orders at me, a text from Guvnah came through. I couldn't read it but I saw his name pop up on the screen. I noticed that the message was quite long before it disappeared into my new messages folder. My heart began to race for sure. However, the Holy Spirit instructed me to focus on the warfare at hand and to leave the text alone. There was too much going on for me to even consider disobedience. In-stead, I whispered, "I trust you, God." Whew! We are here.

The Enemy's Territory

I was pleasantly surprised. Samantha lived in a mid-dle-class neighborhood. It was very well kept and quiet. She had beautiful sunflowers planted in the front yard and hell on the inside. What really caught my attention were the columns on her spacious porch. They were draped with heavenly fabric. I was in antebellum heaven. Opal interrupted my love af-fair by informing me of what I already knew but wanted to escape for just a few seconds, the atmos-phere was thick with warfare. I whipped out my anointing oil and anointed us. When I got to Saman-tha, she swatted the oil from out of my hand and it plummeted to the ground. Opal retrieved it as I bound every occult power daring to challenge the power of God and finished anointing her.

Ha! I'm such a bad mom. It totally escaped my mind that Opal was dog sitting for me. She remind-ed me to get Scout from her car while she attended to Grier. I grabbed Scout from out of Opal's car. She was excited to see me and I was equally excited to see her. Scout was my Maltipoo warrior dog. I took her everywhere that I went. Time after time, I watched God use her to bring comfort and peace to others. I bet she has a divine role to play today. We shall see. Before entering the house, we prayed a prayer of coverage and protection over Scout and ourselves. Scout had to be included in prayer be-cause dark powers will strike your animals. When we entered the home, my head began to ache. I knew that I had entered the enemy's territory. Wisdom in-structed me to have Samantha make a list of what needed to go ahead of time. From the looks of things, she was in no coherent position to instruct.

Opal stands six feet tall and has a head full of beautiful gray locs that compliment her olive skin. They fit her well and exude wisdom long before she speaks. When she speaks, everyone listens. Opal is the kind of assistant who thinks ahead. I looked over and she was pulling construction-quality trash bags from her purse. She knew where the closest dump was and had her husband on standby with their truck just in case anything large needed to be moved. Before going any further, I walked Samantha through several prayers of renunciation designed to break her dark covenants with the occult. The mani-festations were expectedly violent. Powers shook her excessively, they cursed at us, they told dark family secrets, they exposed their plans for her life and they threatened us. Through it all, we stood our ground through Christ Jesus, and one by one, kingdom by kingdom, they left. Occult powers are strong and brutal. Samantha was exhausted to the point that she passed out. We allowed her to rest while we contin-ued to pray.

Behind Closed Doors

I gave Opal the list that Samantha made and she proceeded to retrieve everything that she could find and trash it. What astonished me is that everything demonic was in her bedroom. The entire house was beautifully decorated and filled with color and life. However, her room was a shrine and demonic altar. It was amazing to behold. Everything in her room was dark and hopeless. Her room smelled like death. The saying, "You never know what's going on be-hind closed doors," came to life. Her bed was shaped like a demonic altar. There were demonic pictures on the wall. She had demonic candles everywhere. In the center of the room was a pentagram drawn on the floor that her bed sat in the middle of. There was sage, crystals, and several jars filled with different animal parts and earth elements that she used for her various rituals.

The Notebook of Doom

What hurt most was the discovery of a notebook with the names of unsuspecting coworkers, family members, and people from the community who had offended her. She detailed the spiritual attacks that she invoked on their behalf and its successes. This was a notebook of doom! On the list was a church that she did some graphics work for. The pastor didn't like what she designed. Although he paid her for her services, she felt rejected by him and put a curse of rejection on him and the church. According to her notes, she tracked the effectiveness of the curse, and within one year, his church turned against him, many left and the church eventually closed. I cried because I'm positive that the pastor had no idea that she was the source of his downfall. I held the notebook close to me and prayed over the lists of names and demanded their freedom in the name of Jesus. I dumped the crates that held the tiny jars that contained their names into one of the garbage bags. I broke them thusly symbolizing their freedom. I be-lieve that God honored my prayers.

Everything Has To Go

Readers, it was painful observing Samantha's living conditions and tracking the former state of her heart. For example, how could she have thought that a chandelier made of bones and skulls was ok? This is the risk that we all take when we give ourselves over to a reprobate mind. What was obvious to us was that everything in Samantha's room had to go! It was all contaminated. By this time, we were out of trash bags, but Brother Glenn was on his way with more. He was also bringing help because much needed to go to the dumpster, including her bed. I sat trying to ponder how to break the news to Sa-mantha that we needed to clear out her entire room. To God's glory, we didn't have to. Samantha awoke from her slumber and the first thing that she uttered was, "Everything in my room must go. We can't leave anything." I smiled and Opal began to speak in tongues and prophesied over Samantha's life. The power of God came into the room like fire and the heaviness lifted. We rejoiced as we watched Brother Glenn and the other brothers from church take the enemy's property from out of the room.

The Pentegram

We were undecided about what to do about the pen-tagram. We were relieved to find out that it was a stick-and-peel pentagram. So, we all surrounded it and broke its power from over that atmosphere and closed the demonic portal. We were ready to anoint the house but Brother Glenn communicated that he discerned that it was not time yet. We all paused and came into agreement with what the Holy Spirit im-pressed upon him. We agreed to wait on God for fur-ther instructions. Brother Glenn and crew left to dump everything and to buy white paint for Saman-tha's walls. The hideous black walls had to go. They also picked up a new chandelier for her bedroom. Obviously, the one that was in there was straight from hell.

One thing that I learned a long time ago is that in order to be effective in this type of ministry, you need a solid team where there is trust and everyone knows their role and gifts. There is no way that I could have helped Samantha alone. There are so many layers to her story. Long after today, she will need to be discipled and receive many layers of inner therapy. Even so, our girl with the pink hair is well on her way. She's asleep again and I can't blame her because experiencing deliverance for some is abso-lutely draining.

The Battle is Not Yours

I heard the Holy Spirit say, "Faithe, the battle is not yours, it's the Lord's." "Hmmmm, ok, God, I hear you." I didn't know the details but I knew that some-thing was up. Clearly, Opal did too. She joined me in the living room. She walked over to me, anointed me with more oil, and prayed over me. I did the same for her. We held hands signifying solidarity. She spoke into the atmosphere what moments earlier the Holy Spirit spoke to my heart. The battle is not ours but the Lord's. I felt like I was part Spartan. A Holy boldness came upon us. I looked at Opal and spiritu-ally, I saw the fire of God on her mouth and hands. I looked down at my hands and I saw the same. I felt the flames on my mouth and tongue. It occurred to me, there's about to be a showdown at some point in this journey.

Occult Deliverances

Deliverance is a process within itself but when you're working with clients coming out of the occult, you have to work with them and monitor them very closely. It was beautiful watching Opal keep watch over Samantha as she slept. And with every twitch or sign of discomfort, she commanded the powers of darkness to break and flee. She spoke scripture over her and repeatedly reminded her of God's love for her and that she was no more an orphan. I admire Opal's anointing. She was powerful and motherly. She is detail-oriented and patient. She is incredible. I learned so much from her. She taught me what it truly means to give your life to this work.

Settlement Is Necessary

Opal helped me understand why for so many years the enemy fought my settlement. Settlement is nec-essary for a deliverance minister. You can't focus and fully give your all unsettled. She helped me un-derstand that your God ordained spouse can easily locate you in your settled place versus an unsettled place. This is how she was found by Brother Glenn. Interestingly, when he found her, he informed her that she had a demonic Bae based on her behavior and the ridiculous warfare that they experienced. It was a process but to God's glory, he was equipped to help her fight and evict him.

It's been quite the day. I would have never guessed this to be how my day would unfold, but I'm so thankful to be used by God. When you are called in your place, you never have to fish for minis-try. As you are witnessing, ministry will find you. And don't think for a moment that the text from Guvnah has escaped my mind. I'm curious but I'm focused. I have disciplined myself to listen to God and to address one situation at a time. Furthermore, I already thought things through. Grier's flight doesn't land until another two hours. Therefore, I knew that she was not in trouble and that's what mattered to me at the moment.

Brother Ishmael

Ohhhhhh, I'm smelling a wonderful aroma, some-body is in the kitchen throwing down and I know who. I skipped into the kitchen only to find Brother Ishmael cooking his famous lamb stew. This is so like him. He ensures that we are fed and nurtured during long hours of warfare. Cooking and providing comfort is his thing. Get in view, Hulk Hogan. Brother Ishmael could pass as his identical twin. He even laughs and speaks like him. When eating is ap-propriate, Brother Ishmael always ensures that we have grub awaiting us. Cooking is his love. He was head chef for 20 years while in the Navy. Brother Ishmael inquired how I met Samantha and when I recounted the story, he was both stunned and in-trigued. By this time, Samantha was awake and had migrated into the kitchen along with Opal.

Brother Ishmael and Samantha bonded quickly and it was delightful to watch. I knew that she re-minded him of his granddaughter who died from ovarian cancer a few years back. Although a man of few words, he loved empowering others to know their authority in Christ. He focused on teaching Samantha about her authority over Satan and his helpers. He informed her of the power that she now possessed and assured her that she didn't have to live in fear anymore. He taught her about our three most favorite weapons of warfare, the name of Jesus, the blood, and Holy Ghost Fire. She listened intense-ly. He took his time breaking each one down and emphasizing how to use them. Brother Ishmael didn't have to say it out loud but I could discern that he was preparing Samantha for something that he discerned. I stood in awe of how God was using eve-ryone for His greater good.

Something Dark Brewing

Shortly thereafter, the rest of the crew joined us. They were pleased with their paint job and the hang-ing of the new chandelier. Samantha kept thanking us over and over again. Not that we needed it but her gratitude fueled us to go the extra mile for her. We were not going to leave her prematurely. We were committed. There was a slight uneasiness in the room because we were still waiting on further instructions from God. Brother Ishmael began asking questions about demonic Baes and I did my best to answer his questions. It became apparent that every-one was interested in learning more They had deep questions and I had deep answers. Being the teacher that I am, I was delighted to slide into teaching mode and besides, it kept my mind from wondering about Guvnah's text. Maybe God would give further in-structions while I was teaching. There was no way of knowing how and when he would speak next. How-ever, what I was certain of was that something dark was brewing. Even so, God reminded "my wanna be troubled heart" that the battle belonged to him.

Bloodline Foundational Health

There is a powerful song by Tasha Cobbs enti-tled, He Knows My Name. It's a tear-jerker and a powerful testament to how personal our father is. So personal that he knows us by name. We are not strangers to Him and that's so comforting. We are his children and he's, ABBA father. Y'all know that I'm going somewhere with this. God is not the only person who knows your name. Satan is the greatest counterfeiter of all time! He wants to know who and what God knows and that includes you. Because he's not all- knowing or omnipresent, he has to rely on familiar spirits. He has to search his records just to keep up. Just like God, he's very familiar with you and your bloodline. He knows you and your blood-line's strengths and weaknesses and he uses the knowledge to devise which weapons of warfare will best trip you up.

Do you realize that most of your weaknesses and strengths are also the weaknesses and strengths of your family members; even the ones from genera-tions past? Satan's mission is to bind your strengths and feed your weaknesses. And when I speak of weakness, I am referring to the sins that you're prone to wander towards when your life doesn't come under the subjection of the Holy Spirit. Take a deep breath and focus because it's imperative that you understand what I'm about to express to you as I did to Samantha and the crew. The health of your bloodline's foundation is everything.

Bloodline Woes

Your foundational health is predicated upon the spiritual works of your ancestors. The strength and wealth of your foundation depends upon the sins or righteousness that your ancestors reinforced. If your ancestors worshipped other gods (idol worship) and indulged in iniquity, your foundation is problematic. Your foundation is filled with demonic cracks spon-sored by contracts and covenants (knowingly and unknowingly) entered into with demonic deities. We all laughed at the Sharman in the movie, *Coming to America II.* I'm going to be honest, many of our an-cestors to some extent or another, dabbled in witch-craft and/or the occult. You may not know who they are, how deep they delved, what or who they offered up, what it cost them and is costing the bloodline. This is how many bloodlines inherited a demonic Bae that's married to the bloodline. Unfortunately, this is how many bloodlines became cursed.

The strength and viciousness of the curse de-pends upon what was done, asked for, and what dei-ties they fed. Because there is no light in Satan, those contracts might have been established while expect-ing protection and gifts of all sorts but the fine print demanded the opposite. What does this have to do with you? Well, those covenants remain in place un-til they are stopped. Hear me, not until you come in-to Christ but until they are STOPPED. Curses DO NOT fizzle out. They are BROKEN. Meaning, some-one goes in and tears them down. It is what Jesus did on the cross that gives you the authority to disre-spect them and tear them down (Luke 10:19)! I will tell you how later. Keep reading and digesting. You are not yet ready so don't skip to that part. Chill, anxious one. ☺ It's the generational curse breaker who answers the call of God to stop the covenants in their tracks. Woah unto the bloodlines who go from generation to generation without ONE obedient and disciplined enough to answer the call as the breaker.

Altars

An altar is the actual construct where offerings such as food/goods, money, sexual acts, and/or ani-mal/human sacrifices presented to summoned dei-ties is placed or acted out. The location of the altar is where the supernatural and the natural intertwines. This is where the deity summoned is worshipped and beseeched with requests or given vital infor-mation. Altars can be Godly or demonic. The deity summoned usually manifests itself in some manner in order to communicate its pleasure or displeasure, stipulations of the blessing/curse, and what it ex-pects in return. In the Bible, God exhibited his ac-ceptance by speaking agreement or

94

consuming the offering placed on the altar with fire (1 Kings 18:38).

Altars can be erected for just about any re-quest that needs supernatural interference. Altars are most erected requesting long life, direction, heal-ing, protection, marriages, and prosperity just to name a few. Let's examine the examples of Issac, Moses, and Abraham, they erected altars to the true and living God that strengthened their bloodline's foundation. That's why when we pray we can boast that we are the seed of Abraham (Galatians 3:29). Their contracts requested that perpetual blessings rest upon their lineage, and we are a part of that lin-eage. The new covenant ended the need for Chris-tians to erect biblical altars where animal sacrifices and specific food offerings were made to God. I must point out that Godly altars never included sexual acts, orgies, or human blood sacrifices. Those were the practices of pagans.

Christians no longer build altars like in the Bi-ble days. Because of Jesus Christ's death, burial, and resurrection, the Christian's altar is now on his/her knees in prayer where we need not bring anything but ourselves. Sometimes Christians raise personal altars and offerings to God when they feel it's neces-sary to provoke God to adhere to a special and deep-ly personal request. Even then, the offerings are NEVER animal or human blood sacrifices. They don't include sex or anything sinful. It's usually a mone-tary offering or the giving away of something very valuable to the person. Some may call it a sacrificial offering.

Demonic Altars

I have established several times that there is nothing unique or original about Satan. He lifted God's sym-bolic worship system of altars and of course, he de-filed it. Out of desperation, throughout the ages, scores have made their request to his kingdom seek-ing power, fame, riches, fruit of the womb, court cas-es resolved, healing, revenge, and clues about their future. And yes, many have come face to face with the supernatural in ways that they love and regret. It's really those who are deep in the dark craft who practice erecting altars as I described using human and animal blood along with the erotic dancing and orgies. They are extremely serious and looking to in-crease in power and rank. In most cases, you will never know who they are and if you do, they are usually the ones that others seek out for help.

There are novice or low-ranking witches who practice witchcraft in their homes. They do erect al-tars but they are lightweight in nature. As a matter of fact in modern light, calling the psychic, visiting spiritualist, root doctors, the Obeah priest, voodoo priestess are all forms of raising altars. You put your faith, time, and money on the altar. Sometimes dei-ties manifest and others times they don't. Many walk away thinking that their five minutes experi-ence was a waste of time. Little do they know that an entity that would have never known them attached itself to their life just because of their impatience, ig-norance, and/or curiosity floated them into the en-emy's house. Sometimes the potions and directives work, sometimes they don't. It's all a game to get you to come back or seek out someone whom you heard is more powerful. With every visit and every experience, you become entangled in Satan's spi-derweb of entanglement.

The Joke is On You

The joke is on you because demonic deities do not play fair. They may or may not share to what extent their involvement will harm the person and the bloodline. It depends upon the heart of the person. The more sold out for darkness and wicked their heart, the more honest the deities will be. Sometimes they do good by the actual person in the beginning but turn on them once they are deeply ensnared. No matter how devoted the worker of darkness, their master Satan ALWAYS turns on them. You might have entered his gates free and curious, but without a doubt, you leave with his supernatural mark on your countenance and your name on his list; not just your name but your bloodline's name too. So when your daughter makes her first visit, she is no stranger to the kingdom of danger! For some of you, you were expected even if you didn't realize it. It's in your genes to wander to witchcraft like those before you.

Ha! I have heard several stories from people who the workers of darkness refused to touch be-cause of the power of God running through their veins. They were told that they didn't belong in their establishment and asked to leave. This happened to me in high school when I ignorantly asked to read a classmate's Satanic Bible that he brought to school. I didn't know any better, but he did, and I thank God for that. He refused my request by stating, " No, not you Faithe; anybody but you."

Samantha's Altar

The matter of understanding altars will prove essen-tial when going through the process of correcting your foundation and tearing down ANY demonic altars erected against you and your bloodline. Sa-mantha turned her entire room into an altar and that's why everything had to go. This is a great place to add that wherever you sin over and over again is your altar. Her bed was especially problematic be-cause it's where she met Roscoe and gave herself to him time and time again. Most nights, as soon as her head hit the pillow, she received some type of visita-tion. She stated that in the beginning, the experienc-es were pleasant but as time progressed, they be-came unpleasant and at times, brutal.

The furniture in her bedroom was obviously expensive. The quality and craftsmanship was supe-rior to anything that I had ever seen. It looked like something from the Victorian age. It was beautifully dark and eerie. I inquired how she found such piec-es. She shrugged and expressed that she didn't choose or pay for any of them. The pieces started mysteriously arriving at her house one by one ad-dressed specifically to her. They were gifts from Ros-coe and her coven. Admittedly, they made her feel special and like a queen: a dark queen. She didn't know the specifics but she did assume that they were associated with her coven. It became common for unexpected packages to arrive at her home with contents to add to her witchcraft collection.

I Cried

Inwardly, I sighed because I realized that Samantha was no ordinary witch. There is more to her than she realizes. Sure, she was practicing the craft, but it was never in her heart. They took advantage of her aban-donment and rejection issues. Now that I'm learning more, it's becoming apparent that Satan was not go-ing to let her go without a fight and that was the im-pending storm. I glanced around the room, and from the expressions on everyone's faces, they knew what had been revealed to me.

I excused myself from the room and I did what I desired to do for the longest: cry. I sobbed because I wanted to protect Grier but couldn't. I sobbed be-cause my coaching call with the young lady sucked. I sobbed because Samantha had been taken advantage of. I sobbed because I was fearful that I wouldn't be able to stand against the impending showdown. I sobbed because I felt completely inadequate and flawed. I wanted to retreat. I wanted to go to bed. I wanted to die. In that moment, I wanted my, Bae but I didn't have one to call or lean on. I sobbed because I felt ashamed for trying to help others win in a place where I was struggling. *Where's my Bae? Where's my help? Oh God, what am I doing here? How can I get out of this? What am I doing? Why me? I can't! Just take me now.* The tears flowed harder than ever

Opal's Comfort

"Minister Faithe, stop it right now. The enemy is throwing darts at your mind so whatever he's saying to you in this very moment, reject him. We are here in God's strength and we are equipped to tear down the Kingdom of darkness. For such a times as this are we called so I wish a devil or witch might. We are standing on Luke 10:19 so soldier up soldier. You are one of the strongest soldiers that I know. Have your human moment, dry those tears and come back in the room and continue teaching like the leader we know you to be."

And just like that, Opal left, and moments lat-er, I followed as if not a single tear ever flowed from my eyes. She was right. It was the enemy coming against my mind for touching his kingdom. I am in-deed strong through Christ Jesus. Not only am I strong, but I was also created for the hard. And I def-initely believe in spiritual violence. Suffer not a witch to live. Period.

13 Demonic Baes Types

When I walked back into the kitchen, everyone was waiting in anticipation like school children who are fond of their teacher. I blushed at their admiration and eagerness to learn from the woman who just moments earlier had an emotional breakdown. That's so like God to use his imperfect babies for his glory. By the way, everyone needs an Opal on their team to remind them of who they are in God during their human moments. I heard Joyce Myer mention years ago that she does not feel anointed until he walks out on the stage to minister. I draw from her transparency in my not-so-anointed feeling mo-ments.

Ministry Demonic Bae Attacks

I feel impressed by the Holy Spirit to minister to those of you who are in ministry and struggling with a demonic Bae. Don't be downtrodden and give up and give in. You are especially targeted by the en-emy to ensnare you with a demonic Bae. Don't be embarrassed or ashamed. Lift your head high man and woman of God and fight. You can overcome the sexual stronghold. Submit yourself entirely to the process. You may be called but brothers and sisters, you still have to work the middle just like everyone else. You still have bloodline baggage to fight just like everyone else. You are anointed, but sweeties, you're human. You are not supernatural. You're fueled by the supernatural. Extend unto yourself grace and humble yourself before God, asking him for help. Repeat this out loud, *"I no longer have to car-ry the shame of having a demonic Bae. Help has located me and I receive it."* Amen, now don't you feel better?

Another Barshook Visit

I started my second teaching segment by sharing the story of the second time that Barshook visited Grier. It was shortly after Guvnah accepted Christ as his personal Savior. In the dream, Barshook was angry and flaunted his rank, screaming that he would not allow Guvnah to reject him and serve a lesser god. Grier laughed at his audacity and her laughter infur-iated him more. Barshook threatened that he had several ways to touch her life and bring her to her knees. Grier stood up to him and reminded him that he was a demonic idol and at best, a bloodline de-monic Bae who's already defeated through the blood of the lamb. Barshook's fury went to ten and this time, he laughed and called her by name.

While moving towards her, he sneered, "Grier, you may serve God, but you are not untouchable. You have many open doors. There are many types of demonic Baes as you so rudely call us. I'll weigh your life and determine who to assign to you." With every step towards her, she became more and more paralyzed. "Woman, don't you know that we will snatch you from behind the cross and finish you? And by the way, since you're claiming what belongs to me, please believe that we are a packaged deal." Barshook moved into her space and kissed her on the lips. She said that she could feel his calloused tongue in her mouth while force-fully groping the rest of her body. That was the night that her screams jerked me from my slumber.

The details of her dream intrigued me. This is one of the ways that those of us who do this work gather entail. Chatty demons lie but there is usually some truth to be found if you know what you're lis-tening for. After Grier settled down and went back to sleep, I found a quiet window of time and asked the Holy Spirit to help me formulate a list of the dif-ferent types of demonic Baes. Together, we identi-fied thirteen different types of demonic Baes and how they attach and attack. Sure, there are more, but I believe that this list is quite comprehensive.

Demonic Baes

Wandering Demonic Baes do not have a set target in mind so I prefer calling them wandering demonic Baes. They operate like predictors wandering throughout the earth looking for those they can sexually violate without at-tachment. They move from victim to victim, territory to territory. They rarely operate as a repeat offender. They look for sin, ancestral curses, evil covenants, dedicated property, and holes in a person's soul as legal rights of access. They also assist other demons who may need their skill of sexual defilement in order to complete their job ef-fectively. Their job is to push you down and attack with their venom of sexual defilement when you are at the edge of a breakthrough, be it financially, spiritually, education-ally, relationally, or whatever else that brings joy to your life. These random encounters can go undetected or de-tected.

Wandering Demonic Baes are the lust demons who ap-pear when perversion enters the bedroom. This type of demonic Bae dominates the club scene when certain music is played that demands for very sensual dancing such as twerking and sensual grinding. The music and dancing charges the atmosphere to become a hotbed for wandering demonic Baes to mark their territory that they will later visit. Some they possess in the moment and cause them to orgasm while on the dance floor or encourage them to choose a random to take home. Sometimes it's the demon-ic Bae of polygamy manifesting through its host, inviting a demonic orgy.

Monogamous Demonic Baes attach themselves to one person and claim them as their Bae. This spirit operates in like manner as a devoted Bae does in the natural. In a sick, twisted, and dangerous way, it protects, provides for, and covers its human Bae. It is very territorial and is often responsible for the torment and misfortune of anyone who tries to enter the life of their chosen Bae. If not stopped, it will stop at nothing (including death) to block Bae of any perceived threat to their union. They don't just make ro-mantic threats, they are capable of attacking anyone who can gain Bae's deepest affection and respect. This list in-cludes Bae's children, family, friends, and spiritual leaders.

This type of demonic Bae is more interested in (spirit-ually) building a family with Bae in his underwater king-dom. It's interested in Bae having or producing spirit-children. It's a complicated concept, but this is where the dreams about nursing and/or taking care of strange chil-dren that you perceive are yours usually comes from. I mentioned this before, but I've killed spirit children during deliverance sessions where the demonic Bae begged for their lives or cried over their deaths.

Demonic Bae's legal right is typically attached to a door that you opened or a witchcraft-type covenant that was deliberately placed on Bae. I have found that this type lives in Bae's body and strikes often. He sponsors compul-sive sexual thoughts and various sex addictions. And that's why he shows up the moment that Bae relaxes or tries to drift off to sleep. Their presence can be conscious or unconscious, physical and spiritual.

The Witch/Warlock Demonic Baes are the ones who chooses a person and gains access using witchcraft meth-ods. In this case, you are not dealing with a demon, you are married to a physical being who practices witchcraft (witch or warlock) and has taken an interest in you and claims you as their Bae. Unbeknownst to you, they ma-nipulate you into a spiritual marriage and block you from getting married the same way that demons do. They gain access to you through astro projection, voodoo dolls, and other ways that I'm not privy to. Victims report hearing a person enter their room, feeling them sit or lay beside them. They experience their touch and sexual manipula-tion. Others discern that someone invisible is watching them. Some reported dreaming of their genitals being rubbed to a point of orgasm. The experiences vary from person to person.

This is also how a family member who practices witchcraft can marry another family member without their knowledge. A witch/warlock can marry all of their chil-dren in the realm of the spirit. He marries their soul. This is how blessings can be stolen or diverted. This is also how a person can become spiritually caged and operate as a blind witch. Their presence can be conscious or uncon-scious in their Bae's life.

I'm A Witch Demonic Baes can be difficult to understand so I'm really going to take my time explaining this next concept because it's so common. I have spoken to many women who found out that they were sleeping with a warlock after almost losing everything that they valued. For some reason, this is common in Jamaican, Haitian, and African cultures. Some knew that they were sleeping with darkness but out of ignorance, didn't understand the grav-ity of their decision; especially American women who are easily lured by foreign accents.

Some witches and warlocks choose non-suspecting persons to have random sex (especially prominent married men), date, and occasionally, marry. During the sexual ex-change, they enter into a covenant with them because as you well know, sex binds. During the sexual exchange, they swap uncommon destinies for common destinies, or they bankrupt them of their glory. In such cases, they use their victim's glory as an offering to increase in power. This is how a person's life can go on the decline after such encounters. This is a prime example of power changing hands but in the wrong direction. As you can see, when you break free, you're taking back more than your marital destiny!

The encounter or relationship may end, but they are bound to your soul and you to theirs. This type of de-monic Bae's wickedness can escalate to barbarous heights. Driven by the hosts of demons who live within, their sex-ual appetite can become dangerously dark and sadistic. This is where perversion such as child abuse, child por-nography, sex slaves, bestiality, snuff porn/snuff acts, sexual orgies, drinking and wallowing in blood during sex, and so much more that I care not to think of comes into play. It is a sick and dark world out there.

Sent Demonic Baes can appear when a spiteful person who engages in witchcraft visits a worker of darkness and pays to have a demonic Bae assigned to a person's life. The attack will be successful if you have open doors oper-ating in your life. I know that this sounds sick but jealousy and offense are great motivators to a wounded soul and lives void of the convictive power of Christ. This is a common practice of scorned lovers. Some kill and others use the craft!

This may shock you but scores of Christians prac-tice witchcraft. They are deceived and lack true conviction, and if you cross them, their weapons of warfare will be carnal and mighty through Satan for the establishing of strongholds in your life. So, it's not just wayward or un-suspecting relatives, neighbors, friends, coworkers, and territorial witches who would dare touch your marital des-tiny with such disgusting torment. Always remember, if you have a demonic Bae, there's a WHY & WHO. Some-times that who is you!

Admirer Demonic Baes are the demons or witches that have taken a liking to you. You may or may not be in con-tract. It may or may not sleep with you. It operates more like a close friend who secretly likes you and sabotages any other friendship that you try to form. This spirit is the sneakiest and often takes sooooo much time to detect. Usually, he shows up as a stalker or what deliverance min-isters call a, follow, follow spirit.

A young woman inquired of the Lord to show her the source of her problems. She drifted to sleep and a man appeared to her bragging how fond of her he was. He fur-ther expressed that he had a picture of her and any time that he met a new woman, he would compare them, but to him, she was the fairest of them all. When she awoke, she understood that he was the man that would occasionally appear in her dreams admiring her from a distance. She never paid the dreams close attention because to her knowledge, he never slept with her. He was there quietly sabotaging her. Once she dealt with him, soon after, she was found by her God-ordained spouse.

Bloodline Demonic Baes are married to the bloodline and claim the men and women who carry the DNA that's tied to the family named on their contract. This type of demon-ic Bae has it easy because it's contracted into the family. They don't fancy venturing outside of the bloodline. They are attached to the bloodline and that's the extent of their massive spiritual sex trafficking operation.

I have found that most people who have a devoted demonic Bae got it from their bloodline and during their first sexual experience, they were initiated. Many have been introduced to the seductive powers of their bloodline demonic Bae while at family gatherings or while visiting relatives. Incest is a favorite tool of initiation that bloodline Baes use to bind. The innocent and infamous game of mommy and daddy that kids play has kept many blood-line demonic Baes well fed.

There are entire bloodlines whose marital wealth has been turned over to dark powers, and you can tell by the marital fruit of the bloodline. In rare cases, it's some-times just a sect of the bloodline. For example, Uncle Ray, through witchcraft, assigns a demonic Bae to his brother Paul's children. He captures the destinies of his Paul's children in order to strengthen his children's destinies. Uncle Paul's children struggle while Uncle Ray's children prosper greatly. Regardless of how it got there, when an Incubus/Succubus spirit marries the bloodline, depending upon the stipulations of the curse, the bloodline will struggle to prosper in marriage and in other areas of life. The entire family shares the same spirit spouse. And yes, you can have a demonic Bae from both bloodlines, your mother's bloodline and your father's bloodline.

Demonic Baes collect on the bloodline curse until one arises bold enough and equipped enough to challenge it. Instead of the curse fizzing out with the third or fourth generation, they ensure that it outlives its expiration date by influencing the bloodline Baes to continue the sins of their forefathers. Like the monogamous spirit spouse, these spirits are territorial and dangerous. Their presence can be conscious or unconscious. For a better understand-ing of how family members can cause curses to come upon the bloodline, read chapter 5, Root Of The Matter in my book, You Already Know..You Can't Build On A De-monic Foundation.

Invited Demonic Baes are deliberately summonsed and entered into contract with during some type of occult ritu-al. They have given their souls to the demonic Bae for greater occult power, acts of evil, fame, fortune, healing, or to simply quench their loneliness and sexual appetite. The deity who answers or denies their requests, marries them. Sometimes such spirits are referred to as guides.

Territorial Demonic Baes are the demonic Baes that rests and governs over territories that are known specifically for their perversion. This demonic Bae can strike by right of the region that you reside in. They can be attached to a specific area, residence, church, or workplace by invitation of unknown history or perpetual sexual sin. Some people's problems didn't start until they accepted a certain job, church, house, and/or region that a demonic Bae is at-tached to. Remember, witches and warlocks claim territo-ries to work their craft.

Cultural Demonic Baes are the demonic Baes that natives summons during festivals and evil ceremonies. As the na-tives are dressed in their native attire and playing their native music, they invoke spirits who manifest and initiate their participants. This is how some tourists have returned home with a demonic Bae although they didn't leave home with one. Eager and ignorant tourists who are in a lot of cases, relaxed by alcohol, go with whatever seems cool. The natives usually know what's going on and de-sire to be chosen because in their witchcraft-induced and poverty-stricken cultures, it's an honor to attract the atten-tion of a cultural demonic Bae.

Ritual Demonic Baes can be assigned to a person through spiritual rituals such as baths taken in the river, lake, or sea for demonic protection and rewards. Those who en-gage in such activities don't understand that when they enter such bodies of water in order to seek the assistance of water spirits, they are inadvertently entered into spir-itual marriages. This happened to me during my early ex-posure to deliverance. I was listening to and following a Nigerian warlock posing as a deliverance minister. During one of his broadcasts, he told us to run a bath, add salt to the water, soak our feet in the water and when done, turn our feet in a certain direction without allowing them to touch the ground before drying them. I can't recall what it was supposed to prophetically symbolize. Any who, after obeying, his Incubus spirit started visiting me in his like-ness. God showed me in a dream that he sacrificed a chicken in our honor in order to solidify the marriage and our obedience to his counsel entered us into contract with him. It was hell disconnecting from that spirit. I'm trying to tell y'all, the enemy doesn't play fair. The enemy does not solve problems, he creates, enforces, and prolongs them.

Borrowed Demonic Baes can be contracted from a person whom you sleep with or associate with and they have one. This is especially true of those who sought deliverance and backslid. Evil spirits love clean vessels. So, your pas-tor, counselor, friend coworker's or sex partner's demonic Bae can claim you as theirs and attach itself to your life because you gave them access. This happened to one of my friends. And when the spirit spouse was being evicted, I said, "I thought that we expelled you months ago." He replied, " I belong to James. Tell her to keep her legs closed." She contracted her partner's demonic Bae.

Linda

About three years ago, I received a call from a young lady named Linda. She called frustrated because she had met a very nice young man who loved God and was a great blessing in her life. However, Linda stat-ed that just about every night since meeting him, she would dream of a strange woman following her and it would whisper the new Bae's name. She further expressed that the woman tried to have sex with her a few times, but each time, her spirit man rose up and rebuked her with the word of God. Linda in-quired if maybe God was trying to tell her some-thing. I chuckled and replied, "Yes. He's telling you that this man has a demonic Bae." Linda communi-cated that she figured that was the case and would ask her Bae if he was struggling with lust/perversion and follow up with me. We talked for a little longer before ending the call. I had a de-liverance session scheduled with a gentleman and I needed to prepare. It's always a pleasure watching the men of God break free so I didn't want to be late.

Linda wasted no time. Several hours after our conversation, she scheduled a coaching call for the next day. I braced myself for the worst. When we spoke, she communicated that at first, she had prob-lems reaching Bae, but he eventually called her back. She started crying while expressing that she never got a chance to ask him about lust. He voluntarily admitted that she could not reach him because he was receiving deliverance by The Power Pusher. OMG! I could not believe it. Her Bae came to me be-cause he recognized that he had a demonic Bae and needed it gone. He expressed that it was showing up in his dreams threatening to finish him if he didn't end his current relationship. It also told him that it would bring harm to his Bae if he insisted on defying her. My God!

His deliverance session was not easy because his demonic Bae was sponsored by bloodline witch-craft. She was stubborn and defiant but eventually gave up the ghost and left by the power of God. The man of God wept like a baby. At the conclusion of the session, he stated, "I'm now ready to give Linda a ring." Even so, I did not make the connection and when I spoke with her, I did not spill the beans that an engagement ring was on the way. However, I did rejoice with her over her Bae's deliverance.

I used an example of a couple but you don't have to be in a romantic relationship with a person to receive attacks from their demonic Bae. Remem-ber, I stated earlier that some demonic Baes attack ANYONE who proposes a threat. And remember, the purpose of sex is to defile you, not pleasure.

Point of Contact Demonic Baes can gain access to your life and form a spiritual marriage through points of contact. Points of contact are anything that they are attached to. Something as simple as wearing jewelry dedicated to a spirit spouse. I remember walking a young woman through deliverance and her spirit spouse refused to leave until she took off the ring that she was wearing. It kept repeating, "She's wearing my ring, she's wearing my ring." So I inquired where the ring came from. She stated that it belonged to her great, great, great grandmother. It was given to her daughter who gave it to her daugh-ter who gave it to her mother who in turn gave it to her. None of them had ever married. Her spirit spouse said that the ring was dedicated to him and that he married anyone who wore it. When she took it off and tossed it in the trash, her demonic Bae cried like a madman. He didn't mind leaving her but wanted the ring to go to someone else. It was quite astonishing to witness. That young woman is now in a Kingdom marriage.

Power Pusher

I must be a pretty decent teacher because every last person under the sound of my voice had pages and pages of notes. I felt bad for their fingers. I searched for signs of fatigue but everyone was wide-eyed and thirsting for more. My stomach inquired about the stew on the stove, but it was not time to indulge. And of course, I thought of Guvnah's text but knew that I couldn't read it yet. I did find comfort in know-ing that if everything stayed on track, Grier had landed and getting settled was in the works.

My silence seemed to make Samantha uncom-fortable and she interrupted with, "Everyone, I'm so sorry for hijacking your time like this. I guess you must be ready to leave by now." I didn't have to say a word. Brother Glenn responded, "Hush child. We are your family and your complete freedom is our ministry and delight. We have given our lives over to this ministry." Everyone gave a hearty amen to his response. And there appear that god-infused smile on Samantha's face. It made my heart smile.

The millennial once again interrupted my si-lence. "Preacher lady." Everyone yelled back at her, "Power Pusher." Opal added, "Or Minister Faithe!" We laughed and laughed at her innocence, but I was so glad that they corrected her for me! Being called preacher lady was irking my nerves. Brother Glenn who's known for his ability to keep us on track chimed in, "Samantha, please continue with your question." "Ok, so, Power Pusher, Barshook told Grier that she had many open doors. Did you ever find out what they were?" "Great question Saman-tha. Actually, I did and we went through her life and closed every door. I will not give you her specifics, but I will end tonight's teaching with the different ways that demonic Baes gain access. We have already discussed a few of those ways but I want to be clearer."

Suddenly my phone started going off again. Brother Ishmael was sitting next to my phone. I didn't inquire, but he blurted out that someone named Guvnah was tex-ting me. I thanked him and asked him to turn my phone off for me. Inwardly my heart was beating a million beats a minute. My flesh wanted to defy God but I was nobody's fool! "Focus, Faithe" became my heart's chant, and that's exactly what I did.

Demonic Appetites

Talking to Samantha and the others about the Su-pernatural was so easy because I didn't have to con-vince them that demons or witches are real. They al-so understood that no curse or demonic covenant could enter a person's life without a cause (Proverbs 26:2). In the world of deliverance, we call those caus-es, legal rights. Legal rights are EVERYTHING in the spirit realm and this is the part that so many well-meaning Christians miss.

Every demon has a sin specialty that they are responsible for enforcing. It is that sin that attracts and feeds them. Those particular sins are what deliverance ministers call, sin offerings. Sin offerings serve as food to demons that give them nourishment and satisfy their demonic appetites. Spirits use a variety of devices to expose the world to their various specialties. This is why the Bible states that we should not be ignorant concerning the ways that demons operate (2 Corinthians 2:11).

Demonic Roles

Demons, coerce, coach, suggest, manipulate, and be-guile. They have something to say regarding every topic imaginable. They are master manipulators and communicators. For example, the spirit of rejection's specialty is rejection. This spirit is behind projecting rejection into the lives of mankind. It teaches man-kind how to carry out its likeness. Led by or influ-enced by rejection. Poor Tommy implements what he's learned and in turn, rejects his friend Sarah. His actions excite the spirit of rejection who then rav-enously feeds on his sin offering. The spirit of rejec-tion then flips the script on him and sends more re-jection not only in Sarah's way but his way as well. They then fear being rejected and inadvertently send more rejection to others, which are now sponsored by their soul wounds. And now there's a pattern of rejection in their lives. Before you know it, they are trapped in rejection's web (stronghold) until deliver-ance becomes their portion.

Everything Really Ain't A Demon

Just think of the damage that well-meaning Chris-tians do by yelling, "Everything ain't a demon." Hmmm, everything may not be a demon, but if it's stealing, killing, and destroying, it's sponsored by one! In the case of Incubus and Succubus, they are attracted to the stench of sexual sins of all types. They teach, insinuate, instigate and wait for us to take the bait in one way or another. That's their way in. The first couple of acts are considered sin (foot-holds) but the repetitiveness turns into iniquity that forms a stronghold. No matter how your demonic Bae attached itself to you, sexual perversion is in-volved directly or indirectly. Listed below are the types of sexual sins that invite and feed the Incu-bus/Succubus demons:

Fornication is when a man or woman engages in sexual intercourse outside of marriage. Sex is won-derful but there is a reason why God asks his chil-dren to abstain until marriage. It's for their emotion-al, physical, and spiritual protection.

Masturbation is one of those sins that Christians try to justify. However, it's problematic as well. It's equivalent to a person sinning against their own body (1 Corinthians 6:18). The lustful thoughts that accompany the act further the defilement. In addi-tion to other acts of sexual sin, demons are attracted to the act of watching a person defile themselves and others. As you lay touching yourself, you are open-ing portals for those spirits to come and go as they please. The angels of God turn their backs while the demons of Satan join in and give instructions to heighten the perversion. Just know that whether you're self-pleasing or joining in with another, you have an unseen (sometimes seen) audience.

Sexual perversion includes: group-sex, pornography, bestiality, adultery, promiscuity, homosexuality, les-bianism, incest, and prostitution are all examples of sexual perversion. Some of them are common sense areas while others I will elaborate on. I do under-stand today's culture. However, The topics of homo-sexuality and lesbianism are truly non-debatable sins in the word of God. They are unacceptable in God's sight (Leviticus 18:22, Leviticus 20:13, Romans 1:26-27, I Corinthians 6:9-19). The world has packaged such acts in order to make them appear normal, ac-ceptable and if you disagree, you're being judgmen-tal and homophobic. Good news, the world's opinion doesn't matter. There is a way that seems right to a man but the end leads to destruction (Proverbs 14:12).

You may have a friend or relative who's practicing such a lifestyle and you love them very much. I get it. However, your love for them or who they profess to be at the core does not trump the law of God. God doesn't change his mind because a person is nice and has a good heart. I have found that individuals who empathize with the homosexual lifestyle come into agreement with it and it's often used as a legal right in the spirit world to accuse you before God. I re-member at one point in my life, I started having loads of homosexual and lesbian dreams. I knew that I was not interested in that lifestyle. When I be-seeched God for answers, He indicated that I was in agreement with the lifestyle by reason of what I watched and applauded in the lives of those who had surrendered to the lifestyle. He was right. I re-pented and the dreams stopped.

121

Another area where Christians compromise is **pornography**. I've heard some say that porn is safer than having sex. In a way, yes, if you're solely fo-cused on the flesh aspect. However, it's harmful to your spirit. Without going too deep, let's just use spiritual logic. Why would God ask you to refrain from fornication and then ok you watching two peo-ple fornicate so that you can enjoy an act that he in-stituted and blessed? Nonsense. Please note, the type of porn that you gravitate towards tells if you have soul issues and also indicates what pro-grammed assignment that sexual perversion is to enforce in your life. I really want you to get this, so here's an example. A woman who watches lesbian porn but has no desire to be with a woman in the natural is suffering from unaddressed soul-wounds usually stemming from unaddressed issues with her mother. A person who prefers incest porn is indicating that incest is deeply imbedded in their foundation. This is why they wander to such gutter porn even against their better judgement. They are unknowingly feeding the bloodline sick-ness. Pornography defiles a single's bed and defi-nitely the marital bed. Pornography cannot be justi-fied and is not the solution to teaching an inexperi-enced person about sex. When you open your eye and ear gates to such acts, you are inviting the de-mons behind the acts into your body and home. And you're wondering why your Bae is a demon?!

Sexual Violation includes molestation and rape. It extends an unintentional invitation to demons. I know! You didn't willingly engage in the act so you shouldn't be penalized spiritually. I agree, but here's the thing, those acts defile the soul. Demons do not weigh details because they play dirty. Although the act was non-consensual, the stench of sin attracts them and they seize the opportunity to attach themselves to that person's life. How many cases go un-reported and are kept secret? A person can't be de-livered from what they don't expose. So instead of healing and cleansing, the spirits of concealment, shame, dishonor, and condemnation take root.

The spirit that caused the infraction in the perp now attaches itself to the victim. It remains un-til he or she is purged. If you think about it, if the person does disclose, spiritual cleansing is over-looked as part of the process. Instead, help is solely sought from law enforcement and counselors. That's excellent, but they are skilled at dealing with the body but not the soul and spirit. Sometimes clergymen are notified but in the majority of the cases, they don't walk a person through the necessary cleansing steps. Praying over or with the person is not always enough to rid them of their unwanted guests. It must be deliberately uprooted.

Lustful Lifestyles often go unchecked. There are saints who believe that they are not spirit spouse candidates because they are not physically having sex. However, they think about sex constantly (sexu-al fantasies) and are inappropriately flirtatious. Their conversations are laced with sexual innuendos. When they meet a person, they talk about what they would love to do to that person if they were not saved. Some even resort to sex chat rooms, mastur-bation, and/or sex toys for satisfaction, not realizing that it takes perverted thoughts to get aroused. They also don't weigh that while they are pleasuring themselves, they are performing for an invisible de-monic audience. Others draw the line at fondling, passionate kissing, and/or dry humping. In their mind, they feel justified because it's not like they ac-tually had sex because there was no penetration. Nonsense!

Other Categories of Sexual Sins

I will be the first to admit that there are deliverance ministers who can become very legalistic regarding this topic. I do not want that to be the report of this ministry. Above I listed the major ways that you can become enslaved to a demonic Bae. Now I would like to list ways that entice and feed demonic Baes. The following indicators can also be applied individually and/or to a bloodline.

Vulgar Speech

Have you ever been in the presence of a person who always talks about sex and uses very vulgar terms when addressing sexual topics? A loose mouth re-garding sexual topics excites these demons and it's an indication of what's in a person's heart. Demons love degradation talk regarding anything that God has sanctified. Cursing your marital destiny is vulgar talk. Word curses are vulgar-verbal decrees over the will of God. Calling women female dogs and men dogs are very disgusting terms. Do you realize that in the spirit realm, dogs represent sexual perversion? Therefore, using such terms strengthen demonic prophecies over that person's self-control pertaining to sex. Such terms also partner with their demonic Bae.

A converted heart is truly mindful of what es-capes its lips. When you are upset and hopeless, your demonic Bae will press you to speak against your marital destiny. I can't tell you how many times I had to repent for falling into that demonic trap. WATCH YOUR MOUTH.

A Lack of Modesty

It's my body and I can do with it as I please contra-dicts that your body is not your own and that you've been bought with a price (1 Corinthians 6:19 -20). That's double-mindedness. Loose attire is the fruit of demonic Baes. Unfortunately, the body of Christ is losing this battle. The enemy is using the carnality of pastors and their wives with major platforms to de-file the standard of dress that should be upheld by his sons and daughters.

Please consider that many of our leaders have not been delivered from their demonic Bae and out-side of the pulpit, lust drives them. Sadly, many of our pastors who are not healed nor delivered want the status that their wife is "tight and right" by the world's standards. It feeds their perversion and ego when it's coming from a place of lust. Sadly, many of our broken women of God desire to be deemed sexy. Some of them are subconsciously rebelling against a ridged upbringing and/or the once ugly duckling syndrome. Don't get me wrong, I'm am not talking legalism. I'm not talking about stockings, wearing specific colors, pants, nor wearing attire that may modestly show your curves. Listen, I love to dress just as much as the next person, but there are some things that are not appropriate for God's daughters and sons in and out of the pulpit. A woman of God should not wear see-through clothing nor clothing that exposes her sacred parts or leaves very little for the imagination.

Men who know that the imprint of their goods can be scoped through their tight pants are partnering with demons that incite lust. We have en-tered a time where club attire is being rocked in the church. It's difficult to decipher the women of God from the women of the world. There should be a dif-ference. Demonic Baes are very defensive and will give you a million and one reasons why you don't need to be mindful of how you present yourself.

Christians, we are rocking a name that was granted to us through shed blood. We come to Jesus as we are but it's the Holy Spirit who ensures that we leave that place as Jesus desires us to be. Let's do our part and cooperate with Him.

Regions & Territories

I mentioned this already but it's worth mentioning again. There are times that you can be harassed by a spirit spouse seeking to become your demonic Bae based on where you live. Stop and examine your life, once moving to a specific region, job or neighbor-hood, did the attacks start or increase? Examine the strongholds over the region/territory and if sexual perversion is one, you must war to serve notice that you are not to be played with. Your place of em-ployment can't be governed by a spirit of perversion. You will know if it's the norm for coworkers to sleep with each other. You will know if it's the case by what you observe in the neighborhood. Pay atten-tion. It was in fact a regional demon who tried to stop Daniel's breakthrough (Daniel 10).

I remember moving from Alabama to Ohio for a season. Every breakthrough that I couldn't achieve in Alabama came easily when I moved to Ohio. Per-haps when relocating from one region to another, you should not only consider the population size, job advancements, and the economy. Consider what's governing the region. Spiritual mapping can help prepare you to be on the offense versus defense in a spiritual battle.

Culture

It's the same regarding certain cultures. Africans, West Indians, and dark-skinned men and women have a hard fight by virtue of their ancestral history of worshipping the Marine Kingdom. Listen, don't get upset. Why do you think that our darker-skinned brothers and sisters struggle more than the white and yellow man regarding marriage? Why is the divorce rate higher and filled with single households? Why is Papa "was a rolling stone" syndrome so widely accepted? Pay attention primarily to what we feast on for entertainment as a people. How do our women beautify themselves? What are we singing about? What are our women known for? There lies some of your answers. I'm not saying that we are the only culture with demonic Baes.

Slavery

Slavery didn't help, but it is not the root cause of our broken homes. If you observe African and Caribbean men and women untouched by slavery, you will see that the results are the same as black Americans. I am saying that we as dark-skinned believers have some serious contracts that are STILL binding that must be destroyed. Sadly, there is a great call for Af-rican Americans to return to the gods of their ances-tors and many are jumping aboard. You can't break them for the entire race but you can clear your blood-line from what your misguided ancestors did. And if by chance you honor ancestral worship, don't expect the benefits of the God who refuses to share His glo-ry.

Household Altars

Areas in your home that you have repeatedly en-gaged in unrighteous sex such as couches and beds become altars where you offer up sin. Those offers need to be delivered or tossed out. It depends upon the strength of the sin offerings. Let's say that you committed fornication in your bed once or twice, you may be ok with cleansing and rededicating your bed to God. If you've had a loose booty good time, by all means, I recommend that you throw the entire couch and bed away. You've opened a demonic portal where demons ascend to partake in your sin offer-ings. Just press reset.

For some of you, as soon as you fall asleep in the area, you are bombarded with incubus and suc-cubus visits. It's an easy place for them to attack you because you've sanctified that place and it's marked for easy access. This idea may seem radical but hear me when I tell you, there is nothing too petty for these demons to hold on to. Just like casting your pearls before swine, you keep cleansing yourself and then laying back in the hog pen. Where they do that at? Household altars usually attract wandering de-monic Baes but a demonic Bae can decide to take up permanent residency and claim anyone who enjoys the dwelling place. This is why you may get attacked while visiting a hotel or someone's house overnight.

Electronic Devices

Your gadgets that you use to watch highly sexual-ized content can become possessed and utilized as demonic portals for the spirits of perversion to be fed and strengthened. These same gadgets that you use to send nude pics, vulgar texts, listen to sex-infused music, enter sex chat rooms, sex phone lines, as well as watch porn can send signals to loose booty demons that you are available. Also, demonic trig-gers can be easily programmed into your soul be-cause of what you allow access to your eye and ear gates. Keep thinking it's a game. You can't keep feeding demonic Bae and think that he will starve. What you watch and listen to does matter. So many couples refuse to look through their partner's gadg-ets because they know that they are going to find be-trayal. Been there, done that. Even if a person has trust issues, they should find nothing that wounds but things that heal.

But I Have The Blood

Reflecting on her notes, Samantha blurted out, "Oh Lordy, you are going to need several crosses and a whole lot of holy water for me. I am guilty of just about every single sexual sin imaginable except the animal thingamajig. I like sex but that is my cut-off point." While glaring down at her hands and fid-dling with them, she said, "Whew! Some of the acts I asked for and others, like obviously, I did not. Power Pusher, this is heavy." I couldn't help but laugh to hear her use my favorite word, WHEW. Samantha was the type of person that you could give truth to without all of the extras. I seized the moment to edu-cate her further regarding the spiritual benefits of Jesus' blood sacrifice. Almost yelling she responded, "Whew, so I don't literally have to drink blood?!" For a slight second, I was confused but as usual, the Ho-ly Spirit snapped me back to reality. This young lady was involved in some dark occult practices where she was required to drink blood. She was told that it was no different than what the Christians do. So every time that she heard Christians reference the blood, she believed it to be literal just as it was in her coven. Oh what a relief it was for her to learn the truth. I could now see her freckles again which were momentarily hidden by her undeserved shame. Yaaaaaas, and there returned her smile that could light up the universe. While enjoying the moment of returned joy, the brass millennial blurted out, "Thank you Jesus. I don't have to worry about Ros-coe humping me anymore." I couldn't help but laugh at my uncouth friend. I replied, "You sure don't ." Opal interjected, "That's if he's fully gone. Deliver-ance is a process." And just like a millennial would, Samantha snapped, "Girl, BYE, he's gone!" I dropped my head and shook it from side to side. Samantha laughed as if it was the funniest thing ever before saying, "Gone or not, I have the blood!" And in unison, we all responded, "Yes you do!"

The Prophetic Vocalist

The men rarely engaged in side talk with us. Never-theless, they never missed a thing and looked for ways to serve us. Taking advantage of the break from teaching, Brother Glenn pulled Opal to himself and hugged and kissed her. She melts in his arms errrrrtime he does that to her! ♥□ Brother Glenn was Native American and stood 6'5. His hair was jet black and rested on his shoulders. He was very well spoken. As a matter fact, his voice reminded me of how I imagined Jesus to sound. He is a major asset to our team.

Brother Ishmael volunteered to make us some hot mint tea and we were excited to put something warm in our bellies. We took the fasting process very seriously so we drank it without any added sweet-eners. We always enjoyed being around each other. We looked for ways to serve each other and those we were assigned to. Our bond put me in mind of what the early church must have been like.

Please forgive me but I never introduced Gladys. She's our anointed vocalist and helper. I don't know a lot about her except that she's German and a little person. She's also mildly delayed. She very pleasant but doesn't chatter much. She's faithful and adds value to the team by ensuring that we have every-thing that we need during sessions. God uses her prophetically. Every song that flows from her belly has a right now message. Her voice is so anointed that it demands attention, reflection, and worship to the Most High God. I will never forget what she sang that prepared us for war.

'Tis so sweet to trust in Jesus, Just to take Him at His Word; Just to rest upon His promise, Just to know, "Thus saith the Lord!"Jesus, Jesus, how I trust Him!

Six Witches In the Room

From out of nowhere, our warrior dog, Scout set it off, letting us know that something wasn't right. Her sudden barks startled us to the point that most of us spilled our tea and Glady's' anointed voice cracked something horrible. We rushed to the living room in order to inspect what alarmed Scout. Readers, when we turned the corner to enter the room, I can't speak for anyone else, but I almost hit the floor. There were six witches dressed in long brown hooded cloaks. The hoods were draped over their heads so I could barely see anything more than silhouettes of their faces. They were chanting in unison what sounded like gibberish. They brought with them a foreign and foul odor. It was a mixture of decay, rotten eggs and flowers. I stood frozen but my mind was very much unthawed and it stated, *My God from Zion, there's about to be a showdown in this house tonight!*

The Showdown

The third time that Barshook confronted Grier was the night that Guvnah proposed to her. This time he came in a humble manner. He pleaded with her to forsake her union with Guvnah. Grier said that he was so desperate that he tried to negotiate with her. He promised her a promotion at work, a new Bae, and the ending of a court case that had held up the rewarding of her family's inheritance from her great grandfather's estate for over seven years. He told her that there were dire consequences awaiting him if he lost Guvnah. Grier stood her ground and command-ed him to go in the name of Jesus. Barshook's pride and boldness returned and he threatened Grier. Once again flexing his pseudo authority, he called her by name.

"Grier, you may have closed your open doors but Guvnah has not. Through him, I will make your life a living hell. He's mine and I will not share him with another without their allegiance to me. I can take you as mine too, Grier." Grier yelled, "NEVER!" "Fine, Grier! Through him, I will block you from hav-ing children, and I will defile his thoughts of you. If I have to, I will cut off his cash flow and confuse his vision until he repents, turn from your God, and leaves you. I'm warning you. If he ever steps foot on African soil again, he will never return to you."

Grier shared that the Holy Spirit took over her and before she knew it, she was suspended in the air and yelled, "Shut your defiled mouth demon. I send every plan set against me, my fiancee, and future children to the pit of hell where it belongs. None of your demonic-sponsored weapons formed against me and mine shall ever prosper in the name of Jesus. Swallow the blood of Jesus Christ and die by fire!" And as quickly as Barshook came, he left.

That night, Grier woke me up and this time, she was crying tears of victory and giving all honor and praise to God. Barshook fled and he had given her great but unintended insight into what was holding up her family's inheritance and Barshook's plans to destroy her marriage to Guvnah. Grier was strength-ening her warfare game. Now it was time for Guvnah to level up. He had to realize that he was now an enemy of the ancestral spirit who once fa-vored him by virtue of his bloodline. His devotion to God removed his protection.

With every Bible study, Guvnah was possessing knowledge that could finish the dark power's hold on his family and they weren't having that. Howev-er, he was not yet a serious threat because he didn't truly believe that he needed a spiritual warfare strat-egy. Like so many Christians, he boasted that he was now safe from the touch of the enemy.

I tried to ex-plain to him that he had covenants that needed to be destroyed that were forged by his family. Instead of heading counsel, he got offended and accused me of insulting his family.

Grier, Slow Down

Grier left the states upset with me. Although I drove her to the airport, she barely spoke to me. I upset her by suggesting that she should slow down making wedding plans until things were spiritually settled with Guvnah. Here's the thing, giving unsolicited advice to a person who is convicted that they have found their Bae is always risky. Grier accused me of being lonely, miserable, and downright jealous. Lord have mercy! Nothing could be further from the truth. I was excited for her. It's just that I'm a bit wiser. I have learned that no matter if it's God or not, Guvnah still had to be tested, tried, and proved. We are talking about generations of witchcraft running through his African veins.

Anywho, as quickly as the mess escaped Grier's lips, I forgave her and understood that it seemed like I was just another voice opposing her love for her African King whom she had dreamt of all of her life. Readers, I do not know if Guvnah is for her or not. God did not show me that far, and honestly, it's for Grier to know and not me. What I do know is that Guvnah has a great showdown ahead of him and we will see exactly what he's made of and who's side he's leaning on. At this point, although he's accept-ed Christ as his personal Savior, he should think! There is a reason why Barshook has yet to confront him. It's because they are still spiritually connected. I left Guvnah alone because deliverance ministry 101 teaches that you never work harder for a person's deliverance than they do.

The Chanting

My paralysis was broken by the sound of a thunder-ous male voice. It was Brother Ishmael! He shouted with authority that shook the room, "In the name of Jesus, shut up speaking those disgusting demonic tongues. This territory has been seized by the Most High God." Silence ensued and so did our confidence in our Luke 10:19 anointing. Instantly, our crew grew ten feet taller. Their leader spoke. "We have no business with you people. We are here to address Samantha and that's who we will address." I laughed and chimed in, "Allow me to inform you. You have no authority here. Therefore, you will ad-dress whomever addresses you." The head witch looked at Samantha in order to get her take on what I stated. Samantha was feeling herself and said, "Cheryl, You heard the preacher lady, I mean, Power Pusher." I'm sure that all of my team was laughing on the inside but held it in with beautiful poise.

In case you haven't guessed, Cheryl is Saman-tha's aunt. Cheryl nodded her head and smirked. "After all I've have done for you, this is how you talk to me? You dare betray all of us by renouncing what has sustained you and offered you family all these years?" Samantha replied, "Cheryl, what you offered me was a lie. You offered me bondage and made it look like freedom because you knew that I had noth-ing else to compare it to. Jesus Christ is my provider and sustainer. Frankly, it's insulting to hear you take credit for his work." After reflecting a bit she had the nerve to respond, "Samantha, I'm here to save you. I'm willing to overlook your temporary drunkard-ness. You are very valuable to us and we are not let-ting you go all because these weak Christians filled your head with garbage." I will admit that her insult-ing comment made us shuffle a bit. However, the enemy specializes in trash talking so we gathered ourselves quickly and kept it moving. I was quite impressed the way that Samantha was handling her-self. Her responses made me stand taller in God.

"Cheryl, you don't have to remind me that I'm valuable. I was bought with a price. I have authority over any and everything that tries to exalt itself against what God wants for me. Right Brother Ish-mael?" Brother Ishmael smiled as he shook his head in agreement. "Samantha, I'm warning you!" Read-ers, Samantha was feeling herself and barked, "And furthermore, when the enemy comes in like a flood, God will down him." Correcting her misuse of scrip-ture the crew responded, "Lift up a standard." Sa-mantha cut her eyes at us and snapped, "Same thing." Once again, I'm sure that everyone was chuckling on the inside.

All of a sudden, a force picked Samantha up and threw her up against the wall. Without giving it a second thought, I jumped in between Cheryl and Samantha. I snatched Cheryl's hood off her head. I looked her square in the eyes and spoke. "I wish a witch might." And when I did, the crew began to pray with force! They called down fire and pleaded the blood of Jesus. It was about to go down and we were not afraid. One thing that I taught my babies is that the enemy only responds to authority. Readers, make no mistake about it, we were ready to throw down in our father's name. And I don't mean physi-cally. We were ready to execute our weapons of war-fare.

The Power of God

I could see intimidation arise in Cheryl's eyes and I guess her crew did too so another one stepped up. His name was Stephon. I didn't have to snatch his hood off. He removed it himself. I had to maintain my focus because Stephon was fine. I'm not kidding. He was absolutely beautiful to behold. For focus sake, I will not describe him. Any who, he tried to be the voice of reason and Brother Glenn wasn't having it. Glenn stepped in and communicated that there would be no negotiations. Samantha made her deci-sion and it was final. Glenn further expressed, "I de-stroy with the fire of God all powers that reside in your eyes. Your sorcery has no place here. Holy Ghost fire all over your eyes NOW in the name of

Jesus." Stephon fell to his knees holding his eyes and yelping in pain.

Our crew prayed even harder. They surrounded the room with fire and disarmed the powers of darkness. They commanded the angels of God to do God's work. Two of the witches began to shake un-controllably under the power of God. None of their weapons formed against us were able to prosper.

The Threat of Blood Shed

Cheryl yelled, "Just stop!!!! Just stop it. Our quarrel is not with you! How many times do I have to tell you people that it's Samantha that we want. There does not have to be bloodshed here tonight." This time Opal spoke up. "Blood shed? Blood has already been shed that guarantees our victory over the ene-my." We backed her up with hallelujahs and amens. Opal continued. "I wonder, what makes you think that you have a right to her life to the extent that you show up in her home rolling six deep, totally disre-garding her wishes to be left alone." One of the six screamed, "You sent all of her helpers (demons) back to us. Do you know what she had to endure in order to become filled and gain such incredible rank? So no, we are not backing down or leaving without her." I stepped in. "Sweetheart, what's your name?" She responded, "Chloe." "Chloe, nice name. I have a niece named Chloe. So, how long have you been a witch?" Chloe responded, "None of your business." "Ok, Chloe, I'm sorry if I gave you the impression that answering me was an option. So, in the name of Jesus…"

Before I could finish, she yelled, "Three years."

I responded, "Bless your heart, Chloe. From this point moving forward, I will address Cheryl and on-ly Cheryl. Cheryl, answer Opal's question. What's your right to Samantha's life?" Cheryl responded, "If I tell you, will you let her go?"

Samantha's Boldness

I didn't have a chance to answer Cheryl because Sa-mantha jumped up and stood in between us. She surveyed the room and thanked us for having her back. Tears began to flow down her cheeks and she spoke. "God spoke to me and He said that I have the power through him to stop this. Cheryl, I love you. You are my aunt but you are on the wrong side of this battle. Honestly, it's not a battle for my soul be-cause it's already been claimed by the Most High God."

Cheryl screamed, "That's a lie! Your soul was claimed the day that you killed my brother. Yeah, a life for a life! Your father was the leader of our coven until the day that you decided to play judge and exe-cutioner. Your mother gave you to us when we came to gut her from top to bottom. She begged us to take you instead. It was Roscoe who informed us of your great value and a plan was devised to protect you and raise you up to be greater than your father ever was or would be."

"So yes, your soul is ours. So yes, you owe us. Why do you think that there is no paper or cyber trail of your crime? How do you think you got into college? And who do you believe chose your career for you? Certainly not you! We have been ordering your steps! This house is paid for. The beautiful and extrinsic furniture that you've discarded was espe-cially crafted for you."

"You are ungrateful. It is you who's on the wrong side of this fight. Christians are weak and emotional. Roscoe would have protected you and exalted you beyond your wildest dreams. You are his favorite bride and he wants you back. It's not too late for you. Just say the word."

The Mirror

I couldn't get caught up in the storyline. I assumed the role of watchman and what I observed from my tower made me pause for the cause. At different times I saw the witches discretely glaring at the huge mirror propped in the living room. How in the world did I or any of us miss its presence. I heard the Holy Spirit as clear as day say, "Destroy it." Readers, I love some Holy Ghost-inspired drama and I couldn't survey the room quick enough to find something powerful enough to smash the mirror of splendor into a trillion pieces. The Holy Spirit instructed me to hold my horses. He would tell me how and when. I looked down, and bless God, there was an antique iron sitting next to my right foot. Ain't God good!

Samantha's Inner Child

Samantha was quiet. As a matter of fact, everyone in the room was quiet. I couldn't tell what Samantha was thinking but she was in deep thought. She walked over to Scout, sat on the floor and Scout sat in her lap. She held her close and Scout rested in her arms like the therapeutic dog she was raised to be. Samantha began to rock back and forth. Her entire demeanor changed. She began to giggle like a young girl. She was manifesting a fragmented soul. The Ho-ly Spirit was making this young lady with the beauti-ful pink Mohawk whole right before our eyes. Her giggles quickly turned into fearful sobbing and then angry sobs. And then, her inner wounded princess spoke.

"Daddy, you hurt me. You rejected me. You ig-nored me. You made me feel dirty when you touched me and put your pee-pee inside of me. You were bad and I hate you for it. The bad things that you said to me. The things that you stole from me. I hate you for it. You killed my dog to teach me a lesson. I was only standing up for Mommy. You took her love from me. You killed her confidence. You beat her. You called her names. And I hate you for it. You showed the other children who came to our house more love than you showed me. I hate you for it. I hate you for introducing us to the devil. That wasn't right. I hate you that you turned me into a murderer and forced me to hate myself times ten. So much hate I have for you. Dad, because of you and your evil sister, I turned to a demon for love and power. I really hate you for that."

Forgiveness

Cheryl attempted to interrupt and before she could get more than five words out, the crew shouted, "Shut up." I believe that Cheryl knew what was com-ing and what was coming was enough to permanent-ly shut her door to Samantha. Samantha pulled Scout to her even closer and kissed her head before whis-pering to her, "Scout, I have to forgive them. I have to let them go. I don't want to but it's what God re-quires and I want to please him. I don't want to carry this poison anymore. Scout will you help me?" To our amazement, Scout looked into her eyes as if she understood every single word that flowed from Sa-mantha's lips. She raised up and kissed her on her right cheek. Samantha sobbed the hardest that I had observed since meeting her and when she was done, she uttered, "Dad, Mom, and Aunt Cheryl, I forgive you for all of the pain that you've caused me. This day, from the bottom of my soul, I release you and the pain and replace it with God's love and for-giveness."

She burped a deep burp and yawned a wide yawn. Those actions were without a doubt demons exiting her body. Without being prompted, she re-leased Scout and yelled, "Strongman of murder, leave me now and take anger with you." And when she did, she fell backwards and let out a scream that signaled murder and anger's rebellion against exit-ing. We all knew that they were the last to go. Broth-er Ishmael and Opal ran to her side and ensured that her temple was completely free while the rest of us prayed.

Now

Cheryl and her crew stood silently watching in de-feat. I was still in watchman mode and I observed Stephon glance at the mirror. And when Cheryl thought that no one was paying attention, she glanced at the mirror and then looked at the rest of the crew with a smirk on her face. The mirror was a point of contact and a monitoring device. It was also a portal and it gave me great pleasure to destroy it. So you already know that it gave me utter excite-ment to hear the Holy Spirit whisper, "Now." Y'all I mustered up all of my power pusher strength and hurled the wrought iron into the mirror, shattering it with great force. Cheryl looked at me with evil pro-truding from her eyes and she spewed, "You evil b..." Brother Glenn interjected with, "No Dear. That would be you."Samantha rose from her place of slumber and commanded Cheryl and the gang to leave her home and never to return. Surprisingly, Cheryl dropped her head and without uttering an-other word, made an exit for the door and her crew followed. We all fell to our knees and gave God praise. Scout ran from person to person, instigating praise for doing her part!

The Red Envelope

Brother Ishmael later inquired about the mirror. He was curious. Samantha confirmed that it came with the house. The house was bought for Samantha with insurance money that Cheryl collected from Saman-tha's mother after her father's murder. Apparently, the mirror was placed there by Cheryl so that she could come and go as she and the others pleased. To this very day, we argue that they entered the house through the mirror because the doors were locked. At the end of the day, it really doesn't matter. They left through the front door and they will never more return.

We spent the rest of the night anointing Saman-tha's house. We concluded by feasting on the awe-some soup that Brother Ishmael made and it was scrumptious. Gladys sang her heart out. She whaled "You Have Won Again" by Zacardi Cortez. We cele-brated Jesus! Samantha tried to send us home but we refused. We couldn't leave her alone after such an intense battle. Actually, she wanted us to stay but felt that she was asking too much. We camped out like it was camp meeting time. She took her bedroom and Opal and I took the other two. Everyone else grabbed their inflatable mattresses and found a com-fortable spot to crash. The plan was to rest, consume breakfast and spend as much time as needed devising a plan of discipleship.

I expected sleep to hit me as soon as my head touched the pillow but it did not. I had text messages to read. I reasoned that if I was able to wait this long what was more hours of waiting going to hurt. I asked the Holy Spirit to rock me to sleep in perfect peace and he did just that. I was not being selfish but rather, exhibiting self-care. I was tired and did not need to exude any more energy without recharging.

The next morning Opal was the first to arise. I didn't budge until I smelled fresh coffee. By this time it was 10:30 a.m., I couldn't believe that I had slept that long but it felt great. Everyone reported that they slept well. Scout slipped into Samantha's room and spent the night guarding her. After break-fast, I grabbed a shower and made my way into the living room to hang with the crew. We recounted the events of the previous evening and devised a for-ward plan. We also decided that we would use the next couple of months to learn more about demonic Baes. Don't worry reader, I'm not leaving you out. You can join us in volume two. That's where I'll dis-cuss the signs and symptoms and how to eradicate them.

The Texts

I finally retrieved my phone and turned it on. I took several deep breaths while waiting for it to power up and load. I had several messages from my son, Tyler. I had several messages from Guvnah and two from Grier. I read Tyler's messages and they were pleas-ant and funny. After texting him back, I opened Guvnah's texts and they read:

2:57 pm: *Faithe, I'm in trouble. I underestimated my abil-ity to convince my family to convert to Christianity. I have greatly offended everyone with my truth. My family has threatened to disown me if I don't renounce God. Baba told me that he can't be held responsible for how Barshook deals with me. I'm concerned.*

4:30 pm: *Faithe, I pray that you are not ignoring my plea for help. I have left the family land and am headed to get a hotel. I will bring Grier here with me after I pick her up from the airport. My family refuses to meet her. She is not welcomed to visit my family land.*

7:30 pm: *Faithe, this is Grier. Have you by chance heard from Guvnah? I'm at the airport and I've been waiting for over two hours and he's not here.*

10:42 pm: *I am at a hotel. Guvnah never came for me. I am devastated. I don't know what to do. You promised to be there for me but you too have vanished. I'm afraid.*

9:00 am: *Are you there? I'm sorry for the things that I said to you out of anger. You were right. I have not heard from Guvnah. I'm afraid. Where are you? Why are you ignoring me?*

My Resolve

Sigh. I understood perfectly why the Holy Spirit in-structed me not to read my incoming texts earlier. Guvnah nor Grier weighed my counsel. Now, while hundreds of thousands of miles away, they wanted to draw me into their crisis. I was not obligated to be at their beck and call. I was surprised by my resolve. Maybe because I knew that God was in control and ultimately, Grier and Guvnah were in His hands. Although all of their texts were sent with urgency, I sensed the peace of God. When I shared the texts with the Opal, she sensed the same, peace. Opal and I prayed over Guvnah and Grier. After prayer, Opal encouraged me to call Grier. I tried several times, but she did not answer. My texts went unaddressed as well. Still, I sensed God's peace.

Samantha's Aftercare

I sat on the floor in Indian style and, of course, Scout ran to my side. I glanced up and Brother Glenn was staring at me. I could tell that he was concerned about me. I smiled and said, "I'm ok." He nodded and went about his way. I asked for permission to go home to gather some items for the remainder of the week. It was decided that I would stay with Saman-tha since I was single and worked from home. I could also use that time to administer several rounds of inner-healing and aftercare deliverance. I was pleased for the opportunity to further bond with her. The crew would be in and out for training and on standby, just in case anything popped off. The men made a list of things that needed to be attended to around her home so they would be in and out work-ing as well. Wow, God! This is what it's all about!

After the Battle

After heavy battles, I dreaded going home to dead silence. Tyler lives with his dad in Alabama and Grier is a traveling nurse so she's rarely at home, and when she is, she's playing catch-up with Guvnah. Miss Scout is beautiful company and com-fort but she's a dog. No offense dog lovers. I grabbed my mail and made my way into my cozy abode. I checked messages, answered emails, and proceeded to pack. When done, I flopped down on my plush and inviting bed. I was emotionally exhausted and a bit desiring of some special companionship. I had no one to talk to about all that occurred. No one was there to hold me or help me relax. No one special was there to help shift my mind to something fun and thrilling. Even so, I said, "God, if I never get married again, I am going to forever trust and serve you. Period."

He Spoke to Me

God spoke. God spoke to me. He said, "Faithe, I am a covenant-keeping God. I have answered every pray-er that you've placed before me and presenting you with one of my sons is no exception. You asked me for Kingdom and it's been before you for a while but you've not been able to recognize him. " With tears flowing down my cheeks, I looked down at my pile of mail, and sitting on top was a beautiful red envelope addressed to me. Oh wow! It is from my former Bae that I wrote about earlier. You know, the one who got the taste slapped from out of his mouth! How did he find my address? Thirty-two years later, what on earth could he want? I wasn't sure but I had butterflies in the pit of my stomach. My hands trem-bled as I opened the envelope. The very first line grabbed my attention and instantly convicted my heart that my Kingdom Bae had arrived. Simultane-ously, I received a text from Grier stating, "I am fine but Guvnah has been arrested."

The Power Pusher would like to invite you to connect with her on her Facebook, Twit-ter, and Instagram accounts. For more in-formation regarding upcoming classes, private services, and ministry invites, please visit:

www.thepowerpusher.org

www.ingramcontent.com/pod-product-compliance
Lightning Source LLC
Chambersburg PA
CBHW060351090426
42734CB00011B/2107